SELECTIONS FROM RĀMACANDRIKĀ OF KEŚAVADĀSA

Note on the Painting on the Jacket (*Front*)

Sītā and Lakṣmaṇa in the Forest

It is narrated in the *Rāmāyaṇa* that when Prince Rāma, his wife Sītā, and his brother Lakṣmaṇa were in exile in the forest, the demon Mārīca, instigated by his relation the demon king Rāvaṇa, appeared before them in the shape of a golden deer. Sītā insisted on having that lovely creature as a pet. Rāma suspected that it was a demon in disguise, but reluctantly went in pursuit to please Sītā. The wily deer led him far away into the forest. When Rāma could not catch it alive he shot it with an arrow. Mārīca died crying with a voice imitating that of Rāma, 'O, brother Lakṣmaṇa, I am dying !' When Sītā heard this cry she urged Lakṣmaṇa to go to Rāma's rescue. Lakṣmaṇa tried to convince Sītā that Rāma could not be in danger and that the cry must be the stratagem of some demon. But Sītā still urged him to go, imputing improper motive for his reluctance. When Lakṣmaṇa was thus compelled to leave her alone, Rāvaṇa appeared before her cottage in the guise of a mendicant, and while she was in the act of giving her alms, carried her off. The subject of the painting is Sītā rebuking Lakṣmaṇa.

Note on the Painting on the Jacket (*Back*)

The painting is based on a sculpture in a Hindu cave temple, and shows Rāma marching at the head of his army to fight the demon king Rāvaṇa who had carried off his wife, Sītā, and was holding her captive in his kingdom of Laṅkā.

Selections from Rāmacandrikā of Keśavadāsa

Translated into English Verse

by

K.P. BAHADUR

MOTILAL BANARSIDASS
Delhi :: Varanasi :: Patna

Indological Publishers & Booksellers
Head Office : A. ULLAH MARG, JAWAHAR NAGAR, DELHI-7
Branches : 1. CHOWK, VARANASI-1 (U.P.)
2. ASHOK RAJPATH, PATNA-4 (BIHAR)

UNESCO COLLECTION OF REPRESENTATIVE WORKS
INDIAN SERIES

This Book has been accepted in the Indian Series of the Translations Collection of the United Nations Educational, Scientific and Cultural Organisation (UNESCO)

ISBN 0 8426 914 8

First Edition : Delhi, 1976

Printed in India
BY SHANTILAL JAIN, AT SHRI JAINENDRA PRESS, A-45, PHASE-I, INDUSTRIAL AREA, NARAINA, NEW DELHI-28 AND PUBLISHED BY SUNDARLAL JAIN, FOR MOTILAL BANARSIDASS, A. ULLAH MARG, JAWAHAR NAGAR, DELHI-7

DEDICATION

This book is dedicated to my late father, Sri Iqbal Bahadur.

'Yet in these ears, till hearing dies,
One set slow bell will seem to toll
The passing of the sweetest soul
That ever looked with human eyes.'

Tennyson, *In Memoriam*, *LVI*:3

A Note on Translation of Poetry

'The task of translating poetry is notoriously difficult. It is compounded in the case of the modern idiom which seeks to depart from conventional forms and ordinary syntax.'

—*Edward W. Poitras*

I am greatly indebted to Mr Milton Rosenthal of the UNESCO (Division of Cultural Development) for introducing to me some specimens of verse translations which conform to the 'revolution in poetic taste' which has been going on as he says 'in the field of English poetry in the United States and in Great Britain during the past thirty or more years, though in an especially accelerated form in the last ten years'. This change in taste is bound to create problems for the translator especially when rendering Hindi verse into English. Mr Leonard Nathan of the Department of Rhetoric, University of California, has made some extremely forceful and pertinent observations on this aspect of the problem :

'Modern Hindi has little linguistic similarity to English or to any other Western language, though like German, it locates its verbs at the end of clauses. While Hindi is a member of the Indo-European family, it shares characteristics with other linguistic families of the Indian subcontinent, for instance, Dravidian, as in its use of the postposition. Where English speakers would say : "by the gate," the Hindi speaker says : "gate by." This characteristic, along with innumerable others, makes the job of translation into English a pursuit of equivalences where few exist. The difficulties are made more acute because Hindi prosody accentuates differences already inherent in the two languages. For instance, Hindi verse very often has, at least to the Western ear, a strong trochaic beat, a fact which automatically disqualifies it as modern by our standards that declare any strongly stressed metre, even the common iambic, to be unpoetic affectation.'*

---

* *Poems by Agyeya* translation by S. Vatsyayana and Leonard Nathan (A Note on the Translation).

The task of the translator of much of Hindi verse is to bridge the big gap between the old conventional style which seems to be still popular in Eastern countries and at any rate in India, and the modern taste which Mr Nathan aptly calls 'today's heavily colloquial, deliberately idiosyncratic verse'. While conventional verse having a Miltonic ring about it would be welcomed by Indian readers of English it would fail to qualify in Western countries. Two versions would be impracticable because of the tremendous cost and labour involved. Perhaps an example might make this clearer. Here is an excerpt from a translation of Tulsīdāsa's *Rāmāyaṇa* by S.P. Bahadur.

> 'Creepers entwined in lofty trees,
> Appear like lovely canopies.
> The tall plantain and high palm trees
> Like flags and banners in the breeze.
>
> Those who are careful and keep calm
> Distraction does not them alarm.
> The trees are overlaid with flowers
> Like archers dressed await the hours.'*

This is the old conventional verse with metre and rhyme. Here is anothor example, this time of a translation from the Chinese poet Li Ch'ing-Chao, in modern style.

Ride in the swing
                    over
she stands up
                    languid flexing delicate hands
Multitudinous dew
                    on thin flower
a mist of sweat
                    dampens
                    her light dress through.

The style is revolutionary. There is no rhyme and the metre is irregular. It is what might by called 'free verse', cutting across conventions even to the extent of isolating words and

---

* *The Ramayana of Goswami Tulsidas*, Bahadur S.P., Jaico Publishing House Bombay 1972 (From the Book of Forests).

PRONUNCIATION OF VERNACULAR WORDS

a stands for अ and sounds like *o* in *come*

ā stands for आ and sounds like *a* in *far*

i stands for इ and sounds like *i* in *big*.

ī stands for ई and sounds like *ee* in *feel*

u stands for उ and sounds like *u* in *full*

ū stands for ऊ and sounds like *oo* in *cool*

e stands for ए and sounds like *a* in *brave*

o stands for ओ and sounds like *o* in *moan*

ṛ stands for ड़ and is pronounced with the tongue touching the upper palate

ṇ stands for ण and is also pronounced with the tongue touching the upper palate

t and d stand for त and द and are soft as in French

ṭ and ḍ stand for ट and ड and are hard like *t* and *d* in English

ṁ stands for ं (*anusvāra*) and sounds like *ng*

' (apostrophe) stands for ऽ (elided *a*)

Whenever there is any difficulty, the reader is advised to pronounce the words as in English, ignoring the diacritical marks, if any.

Diacritical marks have not generally been used in names of persons belonging to recent times as well as in well known geographical names.

phrases and putting them in juxtaposition. It is difficult to say which style has more charm, the conventional verse with metre and rhyme or the modern type of verse which defies convention. Perhaps both are charming in their own manner, but the important question is which one is acceptable to the readers for whom the book is meant. Mr Rosenthal of the UNESCO rightly says, 'It is this "revolution in poetic taste" to which the greater majority of Americans and Britons (and the Scandinavians and the Dutch) under the age of 35 now ascribe, which compels us, when translating or revising a work of poetry, to take an initial decision—what public is the translation addressed to ?. . . .If you wish to have the poems in a form which will be read by the young Western poetry-loving public, the final version must have no rhyme, irregular rhythms, and be "colloquial if not heavily, at least somewhat and deliberately idiosyncratic."*

The choice of a suitable style for translating Hindi poetry (as indeed other poetry too) into English for a book which might be read in India and abroad therefore, has its difficulties. I have thought it best to make a sort of compromise between conventionality and the 'deliberately idiosyncratic and heavily colloquial verse' of today. The result is a verse without rhyme and metre but not deliberately idiosyncratic or heavily colloquial. I believe this might satisfy Indian readers, and not discourage 'the Americans, Britons, Scandinavians, Dutch (and others) under thirty-five'. Such a verse would also ensure that the sense of the original is not lost by enslavement to rhyme and metre. Of course in trying to stretch out to both the worlds the translation may reach neither. But that is a risk one has to take.

---

* From Mr Rosenthal's letter to Mr Nayar.

CONTENTS

(Note—The figures denote the numbers of the chapters and verses in *Rāmacandrikā*. For example 1 : 26-27 means Chapter 1, verses 26 to 27).

LIST OF ILLUSTRATIONS

INTRODUCTION

Influences

(i) *Political and Social*

Poet Keśava or Keśavadāsa lived in the age of the Mughal kings—Akbar and Jahāngīr, a period of Indian history which was renowned for grandeur and cultural development. Both these Emperors were liberal in their outlook and tolerant of the religious beliefs of others. Akbar tried to achieve Hindu-Muslim unity by various measures, like abolition of the hated *jiziyā* tax on Hindus, and observance of Hindu rites and ceremonies. He even married Hindu wives, adopted Hindu manners and customs and way of dressing, and shunned meat. Hindu poets like Sūradās, and musicians like Tānasen came to his court, and he got the *Rāmāyaṇa* and *Mahābhārata* translated into Persian. He erected a 'House of Worship' in which discourses were held on all religions in a free and fearless manner. In fact Akbar was somewhat of a mystic himself, and it is recorded by both Badāunī and Abul Fazl that when he was thirty-six years old he underwent such an experience, and he prohibited hunting at that time. Jahāngīr, too, patronised art and literature like his father, Akbar. It is said that he ordered a collection to be made of Sūradās's poems, and contributed one gold *mohur* for every hymn. He took keen interest in painting, calligraphy, and music, and celebrated the festival of *Nauroz* with much show and festivity. He also observed Hindu festivals and thus continued his father's tradition in regard to religious toleration. Jahāngīr was also greatly interested in *sādhus* and *fakīrs*, and Sir Thomas Roe has given us a vivid account of the meeting between one such *fakīr* called Jadrup, and the Emperor, which clearly shows his reverence for such people.

The religious toleration and political stability which prevailed at this time was greatly conducive to the growth and development of art and literature. Keśavadāsa was considered to be one of the nine jewels of literature flourishing during Jahāngīr's reign, and he wrote a long eulogy on the Emperor —*Jahāngīr-jasa-candrikā*. The Orchhā court which Keśavadāsa frequented was a replica of the Mughal durbar. Rāma Shāh, who was one of the rulers of Orchhā used to go often to Jahāngīr's durbar. He left almost all the work of the kingdom to his brother, Indrajīta Singh, who became Keśava's patron. Later on, Vīra Singh, whom Jahāngīr supported, was made Ruler of Orchhā, and about him too, Keśava wrote a book—*Vīrasinghadeva Carita*. Indrajīta Singh was a great lover of poetry, dance and song. A number of accomplished and beautiful women used to grace his apartments, of whom the most prominent was Pravīṇarāya, who, apart from being a good singer and dancer, was skilled in writing poetry. The poets who hovered round the durbars of the Mughal emperors and the Orchhā kings wrote about beauty, adornment, lovemaking, and sensual pleasures. The influence of these poets can be seen in the love-poetry of Keśavadāsa, especially in *Rasika-priyā*.

(ii) *Literary*

There were six main schools of poetry existing in Keśava's time. These were: (a) Heroic poetry. (b) Poetry of devotion. (c) Sūfī poetry. (d) Poetry about Rāma. (e) Poetry about Kṛṣṇa. (f) Poetry of mannerism. (g) Sanskrit poetry.

(a) *Heroic poetry*—Although stray works of heroic verse existed earlier, its real and continuous development started from the period of the first Muslim invaders. The verses were written in a connected series (like *Khumānarāso* of Dalpati Vijaya, *Pṛthivīrājarāso* of Chandrabardāi, *Jayacandra-prakāśa* of Bhaṭṭa Kedār, and so on), or in separate stanzas (like *Vīsaladevarāsō* of Narapati Nalla, and *Ālhākhaṇḍa* of Jagnik).

The subject matter of heroic poetry was the exploits of warriors and kings, and the narration of deeds of valour. Wars and combats, the coming and going of kings and chieftains, the moving about of royal camps and equipage—all these are described in it. Often the abduction of beautiful women was the canse of these wars, and so most of the poems have a subsidiary love interest.

Though Sanskrit, Arabic, and Persian words occur in these poems, they are written in the Dingal dialect, which was the literary language of old Rajasthan. These poems influenced Keśava's narrative works like *Ratanbāvanī*, *Vīrasinghdeva Carit*, and *Jahāṅgīr-jas-candrikā*.

(b) *Poetry of devotion*—The devotional poets who had the greatest influence on Keśava were Nānak and Kabīr, because they emphasised Hindu-Muslim unity, and made no distinction between the rich and the poor, the high and the low. Keśava's native state of Bundelkhand was the centre of the creed of Kabīr, and so his influence was overpowering. The practice of *yoga*, renunciation, prayer, breath-control, the concept of the Absolute, māyā, and the eternal *Brahman*—which were the subject matters of devotional poetry, were emphasised by Keśava in *Vijñānagītā*.

(c) *Sūfī poetry*—This was the fruit of religious tolerance, and the Sūfīs, while remaining Muslims, did not look down on the Hindu faith. The Sūfī poets wrote their poems round some imaginative love tale, some using love stories to illustrate the love of the soul for God. The poems were written in the Avadhī language. Jāyasī's *Padmāvat* and *Akhrāvat* are examples of poetry of this kind. Though the subject matter of Sūfī poetry did not have any notable effect on Keśava's works, its style did, and he wrote *Vīrasinghdeva Carit* in the same manner.

(d) *Poetry about Rāma*—The concept of the Absolute God without shape and form was all very well for the man of wisdom, but the ordinary man wanted a God with human shape to worship. Such a personal God was conceived of by Vālmīki and Tulasīdāsa. The *Rāma caritamānasa* or *Rāmāyaṇa* of Tulasīdāsa, which had been written in Keśava's lifetime had a profound influence on the poet, and he wrote a series of poems on the story of Rāma—*Rāmacandrikā*.

(e) *Poetry about Kṛṣṇa*—The poets who wrote about *Kṛṣṇa* were Jayadeva (*Gītagovinda*, in Sanskrit), Vidyāpati (*Padāvalī*, in Maithilī), Nāmadeva (who wrote in the language of Braja). Then there were Sūradāsa and Mīrā who wrote about Kṛṣṇa subjectively. These poets portrayed Kṛṣṇa as a human being, the pilferer of butter and the lover of cowherd girls. Keśavadāsa's poetry, as for example *Rasikapriyā*, was to some extent influenced by Kṛṣṇa-poetry.

(f) *Poetry of mannerism*—This was called *Rītikāvya*. The first *Rītikāvya* poet of whom we know anything was Kirpārāma. Others were Gopa, Mohanlāl Mishra, Rahīm, K[illegible]nes, and Keśava's own precursor, Balabhadra Mishra. The poetry of mannerism influenced the style of Keśava's poetry to some extent—its abstruseness, obscure imagery, and conventionality.

(g) *Sanskrit poetry*—The two tendencies in Sanskrit poetry were love and rhetorics. The element of love was of course the pivot of most poetry whether written in Sanskrit or in any other language. Rhetorics was a speciality of Sanskrit writers like Bhāmaha, Daṇḍin, Udbhaṭa and the like. Jayadeva went to the extent of saying that if one considered poetry to be shorn of rhetorics and even then thought himself to be wise, he may as well consider fire to be devoid of heat. Keśavadāsa used the love element in *Rasikapriyā*, and wrote *Kavipriyā* as a rhetorical work on the rules and conventions of the poetic art.

(iii) *Religious*

The rule of the Afghans which had preceded the Mughal rule was harsh on Hindus. The Afghans desecrated temples, destroyed idols, and tortured those who would not accept Islam. This treatment resulted in a mighty religious upheaval all over India—the Vaiṣṇava Bhakti movement—which took place mainly in the period between the twelfth and the fifteenth centuries. The leaders of this movement were famous saints who revitalised religion and made it stronger and more spiritual. The first of these famous sages was Rāmānuja who discarded the Absolutism of Śaṅkara and emphasised the worship of a personal God with attributes. Then comes Vallabha, who believed in Kṛṣṇa as the highest reality. He emphasised God's grace and showed preference for the emotional form of worship. Nimbārka, who came after him, expounded the system of *dvaitādvaita*, i. e., difference in non-difference. While his precursors laid stress on reverence for God, Nimbārka wanted men to love Him and he believed that this can be done even while living in the world as a householder. Another renowned saint was Madhva whose philosophy is known as *dvaita*. He believed in the supremacy of religious scripture—for the Hindus the *Vedas*. Religion should, he thought, be pursued by all classes of people—even the Śūdras (untouchables), and it was the duty of government to create an environment for such teaching.

These philosophers and religious savants gave rise to various schools of thought, like Rāmānanda and his followers, Caitanya Mahāprabhu, Hitaharivaṁśa and the Rādhāvallabhas, and Haridāsa. They were all spiritualists and mystics and believed in closer unity with God, by worshipping him, meditating on him and taking his holy name.

Keśava's religious views which he developed in *Rāmacandrikā* and *Vijñānagītā* were moulded by these saints and philosophers, and the latter book is wholly a work of metaphysics in which he explains these religious ideas by an allegory. His utterances in *Rāmacandrikā*, too, show this influence, and in fact he often seeks religious symbolism for his metaphors and similes.

Keśava's Life

Though there is considerable difference in opinion amongst various scholars about Keśava's date of birth, in all probability he was born in the year 1556 (Hindu year *saṁvat* 1612). He was born in Tehrī in northern India in a cultured family *Sanāḍhya* Brahmins. His elder brother, Balabhadra Mishra was a good scholar of Hindi, and wrote some books, and his younger brother was Kalyāṇa. From the records available it is apparent that Keśava was married, and enjoyed a long and happy domestic life. The date of his death is also equally controversial but everything considered it would appear that he died in the year 1618 (Hindu year *saṁvat* 1674), when he was sixty-two years old.

Keśava had great love for his native place, Orchhā where he spent most of his life, and he has painted an idyllic picture of it. The men and women living in Orchhā appeared to him to be like gods and goddesses, and the Betwā river which flowed through it surpassed even the Gaṅgā and Yamunā in its sacredness and merit, so much so that even its sight was enough to wash away one's sins. He also took great pride in his caste and believed that the worship of *Sanāḍhya* Brahmins bestows all the pleasures of heaven, gives domain over all the worlds and slays the wrong-doing of kings. Keśava enjoyed, as his ancestors did, the special patronage of kings like Chandrasen, Indrajīta Singh, Vīra Singh, and Amara Singh. Because of this he was able to freely move in the Orchhā durbar and learnt about statecraft, politics, wars, and the life of kings. He had as his acquaintance Bīrbal, who was a favourite of Akbar, and through him he had access to the Mughal durbar also. Keśava's association with Bīrbal was very close. It is said that Akbar, being displeased with Indrajīta Singh for his failure to present the courtesan Pravīṇarāya in the Mughal durbar, imposed a fine of a crore of rupees (£ 55,556 or $13,33,333) on him. Keśava met Bīrbal secretly and read to him a poem he had composed in his praise, which so pleased him that he got the fine exempted, though the courtesan had to present herself in the durbar. On another occasion the poet recited a stanza he had composed in Bīrbal's praise on which the latter presented him with bills of exchanges of six lakhs of rupees (£ 33,333 or $80,000) which he had in his pocket. According to a traditional account it was Keśava who told Akbar about Bīrbal's death. Bīrbal was so much beloved by the Emperor that no one dared convey this news to him, and Keśava was entrusted with this delicate task. Keśava conveyed it in a stanza thus 'All the beggars became kings, and no one remained to take him. Then god Indra (the god of heaven) also became desirous, and Bīrbal went to fulfil that desire.' When the Emperor heard this and knew about Bīrbal's death he bitterly exclaimed, 'You gave everything to everybody but never gave pain to anyone, which you gave me by so dying—so well did you treat me O, Bīrbal.'

Though Keśava had such influential men as his friends, he could befriend the poor also. Amongst his acquaintances were Patirāma a goldsmith who was illiterate, and Chand the doorkeeper of Bīrbal's palace.

Keśava had met his contemporary Tulasīdāsa who was then residing in Kāśi (Vārāṇasī). According to a traditional tale when he went to meet him, Tulasīdāsa exclaimed, 'Send in this unrefined poet, Keśavadāsa.' Hearing this Keśava left, after informing the servant that he would come again next day. He composed *Rāmacandrikā* during the night, and having done so met Tulasīdāsa at the same spot next morning. This tale is false and fanciful but it shows that the two poets certainly met.

Although Keśava was not fond of travel, he did visit prominent places in northern and central India like Delhi, Agra, Allahabad and Kāśi. He also went sometime or the other to Jodhpur and Udaipur. He gives us interesting accounts of the social life at these places. In Delhi he says there were many people who led double lives. In the day they bathed, put on white dresses, and went round preaching to people to undertake vows and austerities, prayers and sacrifice, while in the night they dallied with handsome coquettish girls and flattered them with words of love. People had become hypocrites and irreligious. The Brahmins did not give deep and serious attention to the *Vedas*, and ascetics thronged public places prattling foolishly. People of low castes proclaimed their excellence by tattooing their bosoms, foreheads, ears and waists. In Kāśi, the religious centre of Hinduism, innocent pilgrims were robbed. A large number of men would commit theft and adultery, and drink wine in the company of strumpets and yet have the arrogance to consider themselves interpreters of truth. The temple priests collected huge sums by accepting gifts and were engaged in libidinous activity.

Keśava had no greed for wealth, which indeed he never lacked. He considered honour and respect much more valuable. He was fair and straightforward in his relations with people, and this quality was also reflected in the characters he delineated in his books. He had the capacity of viewing things in a light vein and would have fully believed with Sir Toby, 'Because thou art virtuous shall there be no more cakes and ale?' He was familiar with all branches of learning, as for example astrology, and medicine, and his writings often depict this acquaintance. His association with kings and ministers gave him a good knowledge of statecraft, weapons of war, games like polo, horses, and the daily lives of royal personages.

In his views about religion, society, and the place of women therein, he was orthodox, and he accepted the traditional beliefs of the people of his age. Keśava was romantic by nature, even if he did not have any love-affair like that of Ghanānanda with Sujān, and he abhorred old age. Once while he was passing by a village well from which some girls were drawing water, one of them greeted him by calling him *bābā* (grandfather). On hearing this Keśava was horrified, and conveyed his grief in a stanza thus:

> O ! Keśava, your grey hair have done for you
> What even your enemies would not have wished,
> So that these antelope-eyed girls,
> With youthful limbs fair as the moon,
> Pass by addressing you as "grandfather".

Works And Commentators

Works

Though there is considerable difference of opinion between various scholars regarding the works ascribable to Keśava, it appears that nine are certainly his. These are as follows:

Works of *Rītikāla* poetry—four : *Rasikapriyā*, *Kavipriyā*, *Shikhnakh*, *Chandamālā*.

Works of religious poetry—two: *Rāmacandrikā*, *Vijñānagītā*.
Works of historical poetry—three: *Vīrasinghdeva Carita*, *Jahāngīr-jas-Candrikā*, *Ratanbāvanī*.

Rasikapriyā, Keśava wrote primarly for Indrajīta Singh, but its object also was the entertainment of readers of amorous verse. The book describes the different kinds of sentiments, including the chief of them, love, the various kinds of young men and women (called *nāyakas* and *nāyikās*), ways of lovemaking and meeting of lovers, the types of emotions, places where lovers meet and how such meetings can be arranged, the women with whom sexual union should be had and those with whom it is prohibited, the arrogance of women and how to overcome it, and so on. This book is of special significance to students and poets writing in Hindi, and is an outstanding work on the art of poetry.

Kavipriyā was written by Keśava for the instructions of the courtesan and poetess Pravīṇarāya, the beloved of Indrajīta Singh, and his own disciple. Keśava called the book 'beloved of poets, and the very life-breath of their lives'. It is an analysis of the poetic art, having much originality and showing much scholarship. In it Keśava sought to lay down the canons of poetry.

Shikhnakh is a small fragment describing the beauty of various parts of a woman's body, and also articles of clothes and ornaments used by them.

Chandamālā is a specialised work about the science of prosody describing stanzas of long and short vowels, and is of special interest to scholars and critics of verse.

Rāmacandrikā is based on the story of Rāma. The account is rather disjointed and contains largely descriptions of rivers, lakes, mountains, gardens, seasons, and the like, and the poet's views about various matters like the art of good government, the virtues of a good king, the sorrows of youth and age, and the vices of priesthood. In portraying the characters of the story, Keśava takes a novel and unorthodox angle and does not idolise them. The book is full of excellent and picturesque descriptions—of nature, of cities, of human behaviour and psychology, which in themselves are a mine of scholarship and entertainment.

Vijñānagītā is a work of metaphysics, and was written on the encouragement of Vīra Singh. The whole narrative is allegorical in nature and describes the battle between two kings—Great Delusion and Wisdom along with their various helpers and allies. Great delusion is finally vanquished, and king Wisdom, the victor, reestablishes his reign. The book also gives a vivid picture of society and manners existing in Keśava's time.

Vīrasinghdeva Carit was written in praise of Vīra Singh and gives accounts of the friction and rivalries between Orchhā chieftains, of the wars between the armies of Vīra Singh and

Akbar, and of Vīra Singh's opulence and daily life. There are descriptions of the town, lake, flower-garden, palace, bed-chamber, the playing of polo, and the beauty of women. The duties of kings and statesmanship are described in the last few chapters. The importance of this work is from the historical angle.

Jahāngīra-jas-candrikā is a work of ordinary merit which, though historical, does not tell us any more about Jahāngīr than what we know from the chronicles of his reign. The scene of the events in the book is mostly set in Agra, the capital of the empire. The Mughal court, the city, the assembly of ministers, and the Rājās and Mahārājās who keep flocking to the court, are described.

Ratanbāvanī was written in praise of Ratansena, son of Madhukar Shāh and is the main source of study of the brief but eventful life of this undaunted, dutiful, and courageous prince, who opposed the mighty armies of Akbar and died a valorous death.

Commentators

There were a large number of commentators on Keśava's works—especially on *Rasikapriyā*, *Kavipriyā*, and *Rāmacandrikā*, but they were all in Braj bhāṣā, which was the language prevalent at that time. They have no punctuation marks which makes their reading difficult. This deficiency was removed by Lala Bhagwandin, who wrote useful and detailed commentaries. Another good commentary is by Lakshminidhi Chaturvedi (on *Rasikapriyā* and *Kavipriyā*)

Keśava, The Artist

Keśava was the artist supreme and knew how to use the tool of language to the best advantage. His writing shows scholarship and erudition, and his descriptions have force and novelty. Some critics consider him abstruse, but this is not generally true of his poetry. He has been called the 'spirit of terse poetry' and it is said that if a ruler or prince did not wish to give a poet his parting perquisite, all he had to do was to ask him the meaning of a poem of Keśavadāsa. Nonetheless this abtruseness is the exception rather than the rule, and there is no doubt that in imaginative flight, facility of language, and use of metaphors and idioms—Keśava is amongst the few poets on the top. The ways in which he accomplishes this are forceful narration, dialogue, descriptions, language, meter and stanza, and embellishment.

(i) *Forceful narration*

The secret of forceful writing is the use of simple and appropriate words. In *Rāmacandrikā* describing Rāma, his wife Sītā, and brother Lakṣmaṇa, in the forest after their banishment, Keśava has captured very admirably the innocent wonder of the forest folk who, seeing them go, ask many questions all in the same breath: 'Who are you, from where have you come, where are you going, and for what work? Whose daughter is this woman, whose daughter-in-law, whose wife? Are you all residents of one village, one family, or are you merely close companions?'[1] These simple words are very expressive and recall Lear's famous soliloquy.

Keśava's descriptions of distress and sorrow are poignant, as when in *Rāmacandrikā* he describes Rāma's distress in not finding Sītā in his hermitage.[2] Later on when he learns of her abduction, from the bird Jaṭāyu, it maddens him and he wanders about asking the birds and trees where she is.[3]

In the same manner Keśava vividly expresses the feeling of elation, as for example Sītā's elation when Hanumān brings her, in Laṅkā, her husband Rāma's ring. In the exuberance of her joy she addresses the ring itself: 'Tell me, O, Ring, is Rāma in good health? And Lakṣmaṇa, my eternal well-wisher—the self-respecting, dear Lakṣmaṇa, is he well? Oh, wise and gentle Hanumān, tell me yourself, for this Ring speaks not—O, why does it not speak?' Hanumān replies with wit and cunning: 'O, mother, the ring answers not, for you address it by the wrong name. Due to separation from you, Rāma has become so thin with grief that he wears this ring now as a bracelet, and calls it by that name. So not being addressed by its correct name it does not respond.'[4]

1. *Rāmacandrikā* IX. 33.
2. *ibid.*, XII. 27.
3. *ibid.*, XII. 39-41.
4. *ibid.*, XIII. 86-87.

In a similar vein Keśava depicts through his powerful narration various other emotions. Bashfulness, when he describes the women of Rāma's household who see love-filled black bees kissing the *mālatī* flowers not minding the presence of the female black bees;[1] humility, when after Rāma has praised Hanumān for the accomplishment of his difficult mission to Laṅkā, he replies humbly that he did not act with valour at all[2]; and courage in the warrior Kumbhakarṇa's challenge to Rāma.[3] In *Ratanbāvanī* and *Vīrasinghdeva Carit* the heroic sentiments are depicted, the fearful and dreadful in *Rāmacandrikā* and *Kavipriyā* respectively, and the emotion of gentleness in various verses of *Rāmacandrikā*. The sentiment of laughter is illustrated in *Rasikapriyā* where Rādhā is tricked by the cowherd maidens when they bring her lover Kṛṣṇa to her, disguised as a girl[4], and Kṛṣṇa is deceived when he stops a cowherd girl whose earthen jar is splashed with curd outside but when he takes it down finds it empty[5].

(ii) *Dialogue*

Keśava was expert in effective dialogues which enliven his work with their swift repartee and pleasant wit. In *Rāmacandrikā* we find innumerable examples of pithy and expressive dialogues, as for instance between Rāma and the sage Paraśurāma[6] and between the warrior Aṅgada and the demon king Rāvaṇa[7].

(iii) *Descriptions*

We find beautiful descriptions of nature throughout Keśava's works, most of them as ornaments to his books. The charming description of the rainy season in *Rāmacandrikā*[8] is an example. His descriptions of places and things are equally enchanting,

1. *Rāmacandrikā* XXXII. 10-11.
2. *ibid.*, XIV. 33-34.
3. *ibid.*, XVIII. 22-23.
4. *Rasikapriyā* XIV. 15.
5. *ibid.*, XIV. 16.
6. *Rāmacandrikā* VII. 19. et seq.
7. *ibid.*, XVI.6. et seq.
8. *ibid.*, XIII. 13-17.

as for example the accounts of beauty of Sītā's maid-servants[1], the description of Rāma's bed-chamber,[2] and the description of women sporting in the water[3]. Some of these descriptions are the result of Keśava's personal experience, as those describing aspects of kingly life, while others are imaginative (as when he describes the ocean[4], which he never saw), but all are vivid, picturesque, and entertaining.

(iv) *Language*

In Keśavadāsa's age Sanskrit had a strong hold, and though Keśava used mostly Braja language, we find its impact in his writings, as for example in certain portions of *Rāmacandrikā*.[5] A number of Bundelakhaṇḍī words, too, occur in his writings which was natural, as he lived for long in Bundelakhaṇḍa. Such words are *kuchī* (key), *ghorilā* (peg), and *gaurmandāin* (rainbow), and Avadhi words like *ihāṁ* (here), *dikhāu* (show), and so on. Arabic and Persian words were used by Keśava though in a slightly modified form. Examples are, *sirtāj* (crown) *fauj* (army), *fīl* (elephant) *firmān* (royal edict) *durbār* (court) and kūṁch (march).

Apart from enriching the Braj language, in which he wrote, by such words of outside origin, Keśava also modified words to suit his needs, as for example instead of *sādhu* (a pious man) he uses *sādh*, and instead of the familiar word *veśyā* (prostitute), he used *visvā*. Other familiar words he coins on his own, for example *bāpmār* (*-bāp ko mārane vālā*) the murderer of one's own father (*bāp*-father, *mār*-killer).

In order to embellish his language Keśava used proverbs and idioms. In *Rasikapriyā* he says of Kṛṣṇa, *he Hari āṭhahū gāṁth hathāye*, meaning that he is a great mischief-maker[6]. In advising the lover that if his beloved is angry she should first be appeased, he uses a popular saying, '*tāto hai dūdh siraie pījai*', meaning 'the milk is hot, cool it and then drink'.

1. *ibid.*, XXXI. 4.et seq.
2. *ibid.*, XIX. 22-23.
3. *ibid.*, XXXII. 37.
4. *ibid.*, XIV. 41-42.
5. *ibid.*, I.19; III. 13.
6. *Rasikapriyā* III. 14.

Keśava's use of words in their onomatopoeic sense is marvellous, as for example the verses in which he describes the twanging of Śiva's bow,[1] and the description of the approach of Rāma's army[2] in which the words are most appropriately chosen for their sound value.

Few poets have used the instrument of language to such great advantage as Keśava. As Dr Shyamsunder Das says: "I firmly believe that Keśava has given much grandeur and dignity to the Hindi language. Just as Tulasī is to be praised for plainness and simplicity, and Sūra for depth of vision, similarly, and indeed to a far greater extent, Keśava is to be extolled for strength and virility of language."

(v) *Metre and Stanza*

No other poet before Keśava had written in so many different metres as he did, and this malleability of his verse gives it great charm and variety. Describing the jumping about of the monkeys this way and that when they go out in search of Sītā he uses a metre called *hīraka* with such good effect that we see the monkeys prancing before our very eyes.[3] When he describes Rāma's going on horseback[4] he uses the *cañcalā* metre with the same effect as BROWNING in *How they brought the Good News from Ghent to Aix*. In describing the confusion created in Rāma's army by that of Lava and Kuśa he uses a metre called *nārāca*,[5] while when he tells of the maidens singing to wake up Rāma he uses the melodious *haripriyā* metre.[6] Keśava experimented with many kinds of stanzas, and in some respects was an innovator. It is this which gives his verses flexibility and freshness.

(vi) *Embellishment*

Keśava's ornateness was the result of his familiarity with the Mughal and Orchhā courts, and of his pride as a scholar

1. *Rāmacandrikā* VI. 43.
2. *ibid.*, XIV. 38.
3. *ibid.*, XIII. 33.
4. *ibid.*, XXXI. 1.
5. *ibid.*, XXXVI. 16.
6. *ibid.*, XXX. 18.

who wanted to flaunt his learning in the reader's eyes. It was also because he stuck to convention, and conformed to existing rules of poetry. In *Kavipriyā* he said, "Even though poetry be of the highest order, of good quality, full of good and juicy words, and of excellent metre, it does not appear attractive without embellishment."[1]

In *Rasikapriyā*, Keśavadāsa uses embellishment, as for example when describing the desires of Kṛṣṇa—the ornamentation of disposition or mood,[2] or the meeting by night between Kṛṣṇa and the cowherd girls—the *samāhita* ornamentation, where a work is accomplished by chance. In *Rāmacandrikā* he uses embellishment in describing the canopy in the courtyard of Sītā's apartment, which he compares to an assembly-chamber of the gods on Mount Meru.[3] Describing the tear-filled eyes of Akbar on hearing the news of Abul Fazl's death Keśava says: 'Tears trembled in his restless eyes as the lotus shivers when shaken by the wind.'[4] Describing the Betwa river the poet says: 'It flows murmuring and rippling as if the beloved of Rāma Shāh, being displeased with her lord, goes away mumbling in anger.'[5] In describing the march of Vīra Singh he takes the help of the adornment of metaphor, and describes the king's going thus: 'On Vīra Singh's departure each spot is being lost to him one after the other, as on the rising of the sun the stars.[6]

Keśava's Place In Hindi Literature

Keśava's poetry was varied and significant from a number of angles. He was not only an eminent poet but also a scholar and a historian. He has been more successful in stray poems than in poetical compositions in connected series, and in those he occupies a supreme place. He had command over the language he used, *viz.*, that of Braja, he was adept in embellishing his verses by metaphor, similes, and figures of

1. *Kavipriyā* V. 1.
2. *Rasikapriyā* V. 10.
3. *Rāmacandrikā* XXIX. 29.
4. *Vīrasinghdeva Carita* p. 39.
5. *ibid.*, p. 69.
6. *ibid.*, p. 61.

speech, and in the use of metres, no poet in the history of Hind literature can stand comparison with him.

Though later poets did not follow the traditions set by him or the rules of poetical composition to which he subscribed, it cannot be denied that he opened new paths and enriched Hindi poetry. As a historian of his times Keśava has indisputable importance. Though he did not add much to the contemporary account of the Mughal rule and administration, he certainly wrote with authority about the kingdom of Orchhā in which he largely lived and moved. His books *Kavipriyā*, *Vīrasinghdeva Carita* and *Ratanbāvanī* contain much information about events which took place there, and in learning about Orchhā rulers the works of Keśava cannot be ignored.

Above everything Keśava lived a full life. The magnificence of courts, the wiles of ministers and chieftains, the idiosyncracies of kings and emperors, and the treacheries of plotters and assassins, were all within his field of experience. He had devotion, but was not blinded by it, and did not demur to point out the weaknesses of those whom tradition considered faultless, as Rāma and Vibhīṣaṇa, and yet he did not forget wherein they were noble. He worked on a wide canvas, and excelled in his narration whether he was describing lovemaking or the soul's emancipation. He wrote about war, and he wrote about peace, and in both he was equally expressive. He wrote with equal facility about the march of Vīra Singh's forces and the clash of armies, about first love, about the laughter of women, their longing, their fulfilment and their innocent wiles. His vast experience of various aspects of life made him write on almost all subjects—religion, philosophy, court amours, love, hate, and horror; and gave him the gift to speak about everything from the signs to be looked for when buying a horse, to the qualities of the enlightened soul. Age did not bend him, and to the end he remained the amorous poet that he ever was. He did not like to be reminded of the sorrowful passing of youth, and cursed his gray hairs. He could 'walk with kings nor lose the common touch', and where he had as his friend the great Madhukara Shāh and Vīra Singh, he also befriended a common and illiterate goldsmith. His wisdom kept pace with his exuberance, and he knew how much honour could corrupt, greed debase, and intimacy despoil.

Ati ādara ati lobha taiṁ, ati saṅgati taiṁ mitta,
Sādhun hūṁ ko hotāhai, Keśava cañcala citta.

(Keśava says, by excessive honour, excessive greed and excessive association, the nature of sages even becomes unsteady).

Some critics have discounted him as terse, others have dismissed him as a charlatan parading in borrowed clothes. He was neither. As any other writer he could not escape the impress of his age and times, but whatever he wrote was full of strength and vitality, and in some respects he was a pioneer.

Rāmacandrikā

The proof of Keśavadāsa's permanent and undisputed place in Hindi literature is *Rāmacandrikā*. According to Keśava's own account, the sage Vālmīki appeared to him in a dream and asked him to write this book. The sage gave him the *mantra* of Rāma, saying, 'Rāma is the only truth, there is no other'. When Keśava asked the saint, 'How can sorrow be removed?' he replied 'It is Hari (Rāma) who will remove it.' So the poet chose Rāma as his deity, and undertook the sacred task of singing the praises of Rāma, 'Whose splendour ever shines in the whole universe'.

The book is in two parts, the first consisting of twenty chapters or sections, and the second eighteen (from chapters twenty-one to thirty-eight). Although Keśava's *Rāmacandrikā* is based on the famous story of Rāma, there is considerable difference between him and Tulasīdāsa in regard to treatment of the theme and its presentation. Keśava's account is rather unconnected, and the incidents in the story are used by him to air his own views about various matters which interested him.

The book provides an excellent study of the life of the kings of that time—the games they played, their daily routine, durbars, sports, and frolics. Keśava's Rāma is a prototype of the Mughal emperors, and a person given to sensuous pleasures and human weakness. He instantly kills a demon merely because he frightens Sītā. He fans her when she is tired in the forest. While in the royal palace he behaves like the Orchhā rulers or the Mughal emperors, playing polo, seeing jousts of arms, witnessing feasts of love, strolling with Sītā in the arbour, watching the ladies of the court sporting in the water, or enjoying music and dance. Sometimes he is awakened by the thrush, and then he surreptitiously watches lovely women playing in the forest; sometimes he listens to descriptions of the beauty of Sītā's maid-servants.

Much of Keśava's knowledge of government and statecraft is depicted in the book. Rāvaṇa's adviser, Mahodara, instructs the demon king about the science of good government and enumerates the different kinds of ministers and their advisers,[1] while towards the end of the book Rāma gives tips to his sons, grandsons, and nephews on how a king should behave and what steps he should take to protect his kingdom.[2]

An interesting chapter is the one in which Keśava relates the sorrows of childhood, youth, and old age,[3] and another charming account is about the beauty of the various limbs of Sītā's maid-servants as described by Śuka, a close friend of Rāma.[4]

The most unique feature of *Rāmacandrikā*, however, is its superb descriptions of natural beauty—rivers, lakes, forests, gardens, of the rising sun, and of the seasons. There are also brilliant descriptions of places and things—the city of Ayodhyā, Daśaratha's elephants, the game of polo, the ceremony of *Palkāchār*, and the water-sport of lovely women. In such descriptions Keśava is incomparable. His wild flights of fancy, his expressive, sometimes quaint metaphors, make them uncommonly interesting. Describing the rising sun Keśava says that it looks like 'an auspicious jar painted all over with vermilion', or 'as the dust of red rubies powdered by the sharp hooves of the sun's horses.[5] Describing the full moon he calls it a ball of flowers which the wife of heaven's god had smelt and then thrown away. And again, as though it were the

1. *Rāmacandrikā* XVII. 20-27.
2. *ibid.*, XXXIX. 29-36.
3. *ibid.*, XXIV. 3-6; 11-12.
4. *ibid.*, XXXI. 4-21, 23-41.
5. *ibid.*, V. 10-12.

looking glass of Rati, wife of the god of love.[1] Describing the gray hair on he body of an old man he says, 'Are these gray hair, or sprouts of Death, which is very close ? Or is it the senseless soul which has been pricked all over with dry thorns? Or are they the roots of some disease, or countless letters of mental anguish written on the forehead ? Or has old age put the soul in a cage of arrows, or imprisoned it in an embroidered shawl.[2] Describing the whiteness of the bed on which Rāma prepares to sleep, the poet says, it is of a whiteness which was never heard of, and it seems as if the skin of the moon itself had been taken off and spread'.[3] The flags which wave in Ayodhyā are compared to a devotee standing all the time on one leg: 'The flags are very beautiful and perfectly straight, but do not remain still even for half a moment; and they are devotedly austere because they bear staves and stand on one leg all the time.'[4]

In describing the beauty of a woman's body, too, which was a favourite subject of Hindi poets, Keśava uses metaphors which are startlingly unusual. Describing the naked breasts of Maṇḍodarī, the chief wife of Rāvaṇa the demon king, he compares them to 'two golden balls with which polo is played.' And as wherever the balls go the players rush after them, even so the minds of all those who see those naked breasts move to the direction they are inclined.[5] The pigtails of Sītā's maidservants are 'as swords of the beauty-shaped king meant to protect the vows of love and to refute the deception of ace villains'.[6] Or as if they were 'pleasure-giving rivers of adornment which wash away guile and cunning'.[7] The line of hair extending across the middle of the navel is compared to 'a beautiful creeper of adornment in which the two breasts, having in them the splendour of the entire world, are as if two fruits had blossomed'.[8]

1. *Rāmacandrikā* XXX. 41.
2. *ibid.*, XXIV. 12.
3. *ibid.*, XXX. 13.
4. *ibid.*, I.38.
5. *ibid.*, XIX. 32.
6. *ibid.*, XXXI.5.
7. *ibid.*, XXXI.6.
8. *ibid.*, XXXI. 30.

In this selection from *Rāmacandrikā* only those portions of the book have been included which depict Keśava's descriptive power, his insight into human psychology, and his views about various things. The main story of Rāma has been left out, for this is too well-known to deserve repetition, and in *Rāmacandrikā* this story only provides a peg for Keśava to hang his views on. It is precisely because of this that the book is of special significance to Keśava admirers. And for those who have never before delved into his works it is sure to be a wonderful experience, because Keśava is one of those ancient classical Hindi poets the savouring of whom leaves an excitingly fresh and pleasing tang. About *Rāmacandrikā* the late Lala Bhagwandin rightfully says: "In this book one can find numerous examples of Keśava's ingenuity and deep insight. His preference for description of things rather than for mere narration of a story, is enough proof of his profundity".[1]

1. *Keśava-kaumudī*, ed. Lala Bhagwandin, Ramanarayanalal Benimadhav, Allahabad, p. 3.

A GLOSSARY OF VERNACULAR WORDS OCCURRING IN THE INTRODUCTION

Brahma or *Brahman* — This is distinct from *Brahmin* (the priestly caste of Hindus) and *Brāhmaṇa* (the theological manuals composed by and for Brahmins) and Brahmā (the creator of the universe, and the first number of the Hindu triad). *Brahma* or *Brahman* means the absolute and cosmic soul. This is believed to be self-existent, all-pervading, and eternal. All beings emanate from it and return to it. It is uncreated, unborn, and beginningless, and on attaining it the soul attains immortality and is freed from taking birth.

Brahmin — The first of the four Hindu castes who, according to legend, were created from the mouth of *Puruṣa* (Cosmic Spirit) so that they may instruct mankind. It was above all a priestly caste whose duties were the recitation of the *Vedas*, the conducting of religious rites and sacrifices. The other castes were the *Kṣatriyas* (warrior class), *Vaiśyas* (business class) and *Śūdras* (servant class). The first three were known as *dvija* (*dvi-ja*, 'twice born') because they undergo a second spiritual birth during investiture with the sacred thread. The Śūdras are once born and not eligible for the thread or other initiation ceremonies.

dvaita-advaita — The school of Hindu philosophy whose exponent is Rāmānuja—the theory of dualism. The connected schools are (i) *Nirviśeṣa Advaitavāda* (absolute monism) enunciated by Śaṅkara. According to this the cosmic soul is the only reality, and the universe is a mere phenomenal evolution on the Noumenon. (ii) *Dvaitavāda* (dualism) whose exponent is Madhva. According to him the individual self (*jīva*) and the Universal Self

(*Brahman*) are separate but reside together in the same body. *Viśiṣṭādvaitavāda* believes in the worship of a God with attributes. According to Rāmānuja, God is conceived of as being all-powerful and as the controller of the universe which forms his body.

fakīr According to the *Chambers's Dictionary* 'a religious (esp. Mohammedan) mendicant, ascetic, or wonder worker in India'. Some of the *fakīrs* or *sādhus* possess miraculous powers. Their possessions include the following items—a *daṇḍa* or staff, *āchal* a short cross-stick used as a support for the chin or arm during meditation and on certain other ceremonial occasions, a *kamaṇḍala* or ascetic water-pot, a *laṁgoṭī* or loin-cloth, and a *mālā* (rosary) usually of rudrākṣa berries. Fakirs are usually wandering hermits who beg for their food.

Hanumān A famous monkey-chief, the son of the wind-god (Pavana, Vāyu or Marut) and the apsarā Añjanā, wife of a monkey named Kesarī. Hanumān was of great assistance to Rāma in the battle against Rāvaṇa, the demon-king. He was also a great devotee of Rāma. During Rāma's search for Sītā, Hanumān went to Laṅkā (Ceylon) where Rāvaṇa had kept her captive. He met her there and gave her Rāma's signet ring. When he was brought captive to Rāvaṇa the latter ordered his tail to be covered with a rag soaked in oil and set fire to it. But Hanumān, quite unharmed leapt from house to house and set fire to Laṅkā. In the battle between Rāma and Rāvaṇa, Lakṣmaṇa, Rāma's younger brother was wounded grievously. Hanumān was sent to fetch the *sañjīvanī būṭī*, the herb which could cure him. On reaching Mount Kailāsa, where the herb grew, he was unable to find the herb, so he brought the whole mountain. On his return from exile Rāma bestowed on his faithful follower the reward of everlasting youth and longevity.

jiziyā A poll-tax, which according to strict Islamic law was payable only by Jews and Christians. This was, however, claimed by earlier Muslim rulers from their Hindu subjects. The claim was abandoned by Akbar but was reasserted by Aurangzeb.

Kumbha-karṇa (*Kumbha-karṇa* = pot-ear). The following account of him is given by WALKER (*Hindu World*) : The gargantuan son of the rākṣasa Viśravas. His body, especially his ears, were so large that no human building could accommodate him, so he was forced to live out in the open. Like his brother Rāvaṇa he was famed for his devotion to Brahmā who once asked him what boon he desired. He intended to ask for 'eternal life' but his tongue was twisted by the goddess Sarasvatī and his reply was uttered as 'eternal sleep'. Brahmā knew what he wanted, but could not alter the spoken word, so he mitigated his devotee's predicament by allowing him to wake up for one day every six months.

The Rāmāyaṇa tells how when Rāvaṇa was hard pressed by Rāma's forces he sent for Kumbha-karṇa to help him out. Stories of this 'awakening' abound in remarkable detail. He was aroused with great difficulty, by thousands of men and beasts creating a terrible din; by elephants trampling on his body and trumpeting into his ear; by women 'caressing' him with pickaxes and poles and men prodding him with their spears. Awake at last he first partook of a meal of pig, deer, monkeys and human beings, draining it down with 10,000 to 15,000 jars of liquor. He then went near the vānara (monkey) camp of Hanumān and relieved himself, blowing one or two regiments out to sea, submerging several others, and drowning many more before he was through. Taking the field with a mighty roar, he defeated Hanumān, stunned Sugrīva the monkey chief with a rock, and slinging him over his shoulder carried him captive to Laṅkā. Returning to the fray he took on Rāma, and in the savage encounter that followed he was slain by one of Rāma's magical arrows which severed his head from his body. The giant staggered back and fell into the ocean, causing a huge tidal wave that drowned a great multitude of people.

Mahābhārata 'The great war of the Bharatas'. A great epic poem of the Hindus, probably the longest in the world. It is divided into eighteen books (*parvas*) and contains about 2,20,000 lines. The reputed author is Kṛṣṇa Dvaipāyana who is said to have taught it to his pupil Vaiśampāyana, who afterwards recited it at a festival to king Janamejaya. The main subject of the poem is the great war between the Kauravas and Pāṇḍavas, who were descendants through Bharata, from Puru, the great ancestor of one branch of the Lunar race. The object of the struggle was the kingdom whose capital was Hastināpura the ruins of which lie about sixty miles from Delhi, the Indian capital.

mālatī A climbing shrub which fastens on trees and goes to a considerable height. It flowers from July to September. The flowers are white and of middle size, star formed, with petals twisted and irregular. The shrub has bay like leaves.

mantra A word of Persian origin. In Vedic literature *mantras* are those portions of the metrical psalms of praise, as distinct from the liturgical prose portions of the *Brāhmaṇas*. In course of time the term *mantra* came to be applied to any sacred verse from the Scriptures, to spells, cryptic syllables, and 'words of power' based on the magical properties believed to be inherent in sound. The *mantras* were sometimes revealed to *ṛṣis* by direct inspiration, but many were composed by them after long meditation on the mysteries of sound, by means of which they were able to reduce voluminous doctrines to small compass. Great stress is laid on the proper recitation of *mantras*, for much of the efficacy of a rite depends on their correct usage. A *mantra* incorrectly enunciated, uttered at an inappropriate time, or by the wrong person, or with misplaced intent, can, it is said, have disastrous consequences. Generally, *mantras* are of no practical value if read from a book, but they acquire great power if they are learned through the living voice of a guru (preceptor).

māyā In the *Ṛgveda*, *māyā* means magical power, such as the power of a demon to take various shapes. In the *Upaniṣads* it stands for false knowledge—that which is distinct from the true reality called *Brahman.* According to the *advaita* doctrine (see *dvaita-advaita*) the one reality is *Brahman.* The phenomenal world of nature and the identities of all beings have no real existence, but are illusive, the result of *māyā.* It is the temporal, negative, deceptive veil of creation, the obscuring force of nature and the result of *avidyā* or ignorance.

nāyaka Literally 'an eminent person.' Hindi poets consider such persons (*nāyakas*) of various types. According to Keśavadāsa a *nāyaka* is one who has pride in himself, and who is youthful, yielding, handsome, forgiving, wealthy, prosperous, of virtuous taste, noble descent, and skilled in the art of love. He classifies *nāyakas* under four types—agreeable, upright, deceitful, and insolent. Other writers attribute different qualities. According to Viśvanātha a *nāyaka* should be liberal, grateful, wise, noble, forbearing, handsome, youthful, clever and gentle. Bhūpāla conceives that a *nāyaka* should be polite, bounteous, firm, dexterous, religious, eloquent, grateful, pure, and skilled in the arts.

nāyikā Just as lovers or men of good qualities are called *nāyakās* by Hindi poets, lovable women are called *nāyikas*, literally 'a heroine'. *Nāyikās* were classsified according to different situations and circumstances, beauty and form. Such a woman could be one's own wife or another's or a virgin. She could be young, adolescent or middle-aged. Or she could be in different situations in relation to her husband or lover, as for example estranged from him, or preparing to welcome him back, filled with longing for him, or deceived by him and in a fretful mood. A well known classification of *nāyikās* made in *Kāma Sūtra*, *Anaṅgaraṅga* and *Rasamañjarī*—the Hindu classics on erotics, is *viz*. *Padminī*, the lotus woman, *citriṇī*, the art woman, *Śaṅkhinī*, the conch woman, and *Hastinī*, the elephant woman.

Rāma or Rāmacandra Eldest son of Daśaratha, a king of the Solar race, reigning in Ayodhyā. He is the seventh incarnation of the god Viṣṇu, and made his appearance in the world at the end of the Tretā or second age. His story is briefly told in the *Vana Parva* of the *Mahābhārata*, but it is given in full length as the subject of the *Rāmāyaṇa*. The gods were greatly troubled by the demon king Rāvaṇa, so they appealed to Viṣṇu who resolved to be born on the earth as Daśaratha's son. While Daśaratha was performing a sacrifice Viṣṇu appeared as a glorious being from the sacrificial fire and gave him a pot of nectar for his wives to drink. Daśaratha gave half of it to Kauśalyā who brought forth Rāma, a quarter to Kaikeyī, his second wife who gave birth to Bharata, and the rest of it to Sumitrā who gave birth to Lakṣmaṇa and Śatrughna. When Rāma became a youth he won Sītā at a *svayaṁvara* and married her. Preparations were made at Ayodhyā to name Rāma as successor to the throne but due to the intrigue of Kaikeyī Bharata was chosen instead, and Rāma, accompanied by Lakṣmaṇa, his brother and Sītā, went into exile for fourteen years. In the forest Rāvaṇa managed to abduct Sītā with the assistance of his accomplice Mārīca. Rāma sought the alliance of Sugrīva and with his help and that of Sugrīva's army and especially his general Hanumān, waged war against Rāvaṇa.

Rāma's army crossed into Laṅkā (Ceylon) by building a bridge across the narrow straits between Ceylon and India and after killing Rāvaṇa and his warriors Kumbhakarṇa, Meghanāda etc., freed Sītā from captivity. Later, however, she was asked by him to attest her innocence. She declared her purity and called on her mother Earth to prove it. The ground opened and she went inside. Full of grief Rāma decided to enter heaven, and walking into the water of the Sarayū river entered into the glory of Viṣṇu.

Rāmāyaṇa The story of Rāma. It is the oldest of the Sanskrit epic poems, written by the sage Vālmīki, composed about five centuries B. C. There are three main recensions—the Northern which is the oldest and purest, the Bengal version which has been subject to much tampering, and the Bombay one which is midway. The book has seven chapters (*kāṇḍas*), 24,000 stanzas or 96,000 lines. The Eastern Hindi version of the Rāmāyaṇa is the *Rāma-carita-mānasa* (The Lake of Rāma's Deeds) of Tulasīdāsa which is as well known in Northern India as the Bible is in Europe. Another version is the *Adhyātmarāmāyaṇa* whose authorship is ascribed to Vyāsa, but it is considered to be a part of the *Brahmāṇḍa Purāṇa*. (See also Rāma)

Sādhu One who has attained certain powers. A Hindu holy man, ascetic, or wonder-worker. A *sādhu* is generally initiated at the age of twelve. During initiation he drops his own name and assumes a new one. Generally the new name consists of three parts: the first is the name of a god, saint, quality, plant, animal, or descriptive epithet; the second is the sect termination which may be Dāsa, Nātha, Ānanda, Kaṇthaḍ etc., the third is the title taken from one of the ten heads called daśanāmī (ten names). (See also *fakīr*)

Saṁvat A Hindu era commencing from 58 B. C. It is said to have been established by the Parthian sovereign Vonones to commemorate the year of his accession and his victory over his rivals. Its use spread from Parthia to India where it was first employed by the Mālava tribe of Ujjain, and later came to be associated with their semi-mythical king known by his title of Vikramāditya, after whom it was called the *Vikrama Saṁvat*. Originally the era was referred to as the *kṛta*, i. e. established, era.

Sanāḍhya Brahmin A branch of *Gaur* Brahmins—a sub-caste of the Brahmin caste. The *Gaur* Brahmins of Bengal and Delhi constitute a large class. The *Miśra*, (mixed) Brahmins of Bihar and Bengal claim *Gaur* status although this is not universally accepted. The *Śarmā* Brahmins are the most numerous of the *Gaur* class.

Sītā Means 'a furrow'. In the *Vedas* Sītā is the furrow or husbandry personified, and worshipped as a deity presiding over agriculture and fruits. In the *Rāmāyaṇa* she is wife of Rāma and daughter of Janaka, king of Videha. She appeared in a furrow ploughed up by her father during a sacrificial rite for obtaining progeny. She is believed to be the incarnation of the goddess Lakṣmī born to bring about the destruction of the demon king Rāvaṇa.

Rāma won her in a contest by successfully bending the great bow of Śiva. She accompanied him in his exile, and was carried off by Rāvaṇa who approached her disguised as a mendicant. Rāvaṇa did his best to make her yield to him but without success. Her long captivity was ended by Rāma's victory over Rāvaṇa and his army. But when she returned she was received coldly by Rāma as he refused to take her back for he could not believe she had retained her honour. She resolved to establish her purity by the ordeal of fire. The fire could not burn her and the fire-god brought her forth and placed her in her husband's arms. Notwithstanding this it so happened that one day a washerman quarrelled with his wife whom he suspected of adultery. He refused to take her back saying he was not as stupid as Rāma to accept a wife who had lived with another man. When Rāma heard this story he was unable to bear this reproach and ordered his brother Lakṣmaṇa to take her to the forest and kill her. Lakṣmaṇa merely abandoned her and dipped his arrowhead in the sap of a tree which had red juice. Sītā found refuge in Vālmīki's hermitage and gave birth to two sons Lava and Kuśa. When Rāma inaugurated a horse sacrifice and the horse came near the hut of the boys who were by now grown up, caught it and defeated the royal army wounding Lakṣmaṇa, Śatrughna, Bharata, as well as Hanumān. Rāma then came himself and learnt through Vālmīki that Lava and Kuśa were his own sons. Sītā returned to Ayōdhyā but she was broken-hearted and called on her mother to receive her. The ground opened and she was taken back into the bosom of the earth, the source from which she had sprung. (See also Rāma and *Rāmāyaṇa*)

Śūdra One of the four castes of Hindu society. They are also called Harijans or Scheduled castes and their profession is mostly labour or menial service. In modern India they are rising to high positions and effort is being made to give them proper representation in jobs and professions. Mahatma Gandhi did a lot for Harijan uplift. (See also Brahmin)

Vālmīki Literally 'anthill'. A sage who was the reputed author of the *Rāmāyaṇa*. He lived for many years by robbery and plunder. Once a Brahmin came that way and he was about to rob him when the wayfarer said, 'Before you do so ask your wife and children if they will share your sin as they share your plundered wealth'. Vālmīki went to them and got a negative reply. This amazed him and set him thinking. He sat in meditation till an anthill grew round him and he received enlightenment. Vālmīki took to study but refused to write anything till he found a worthy subject and a fit measure to compose his verse in.

Meanwhile Rāma and Sītā came more than once for rest and refuge in his hermitage at Citrakūṭa on the river Mandākinī in district Banda. Sītā too came to his hut when she was deserted by Rāma, and gave birth to her sons Lava and Kuśa. The sage learnt about Rāma's adventures and determined to write about them. He had yet to find a suitable metre.

One day while he was walking on the riverside he saw a female heron grieving for her mate who had been killed by a hunter. The sage burst forth in a stream of verse. Brahmā then conveyed to him through sage Nārada that he should write in that metre. So Vālmīki wrote the epic *Rāmāyaṇa* in it.

Vedas The primary scriptures of Hinduism (from the root *vid*, 'know'). They are believed to be of divine origin and heard by *ṛṣis*, so referred to as *śruti* (what was heard). There are primarily four *Vedas*—*Ṛg*, *Yajur*, *Sāma* and *Atharva*. There are four main divisions of these scriptures. They are (i) *Mantra*, the portion of the *Vedas* which comprise the metrical psalms of praise. They are the most ancient part. (ii) *Brāhmaṇa*, manuals of ritual and prayer for priestly guidance, giving details of sacrificial ceremonial. These belong to a later date. (iii) *Āraṇyaka*, 'forest' treatise for hermits and saints which form appendages to the *Brāhmaṇas*. (iv) *Upaniṣads*, philosophical treatises which often formed part of the *Brāhmaṇas* or were embedded in the *Āraṇyakas*.

The *Mantras* and *Brāhmaṇas* are known as *Karmakāṇḍa*, or parts dealing with sacrificial actions, and

	the *Āraṇyakas* and *Upaniṣads* are called the *jñāna-kāṇḍa* or the portions dealing with knowledge.
Vibhīṣaṇa	'Terrible'. A younger brother of Rāvaṇa. He got a boon from Brahmā that he should never commit an unworthy action. He was virtuous and opposed to the practices of the demons. This led to a quarrel between him and Rāvaṇa who kicked him from his seat. Thereupon he went over to Rāma's side. After Rāvaṇa's defeat and death he was enthroned by Rāma as King of Laṅkā.
Yoga	One of the six orthodox systems of Hindu philosophy, believed to have been founded by the sage Yājñavalkya and later codified by Patañjali in his *Yoga-sūtra.* Yoga is a form of mental and physical discipline. The word is derived from the root *yuj* 'yoke' or 'join'. Its aim is to teach the means by which the human soul (*jīvātman*) might attain complete union with the universal soul (*Paramātman*). There are several forms of *yoga*—*karma-yoga,* salvation through works; *bhakti-yoga,* salvation through faith; *jñāna-yoga,* through knowledge; *mantra-yoga,* through the use of *mantras* or spells; *laya-yoga* through the activation of subtle centres of the body; *haṭha-yoga,* through physical culture; and *rāja-yoga* through spiritual culture.
Note :	Names of famous saints, kings, towns, and the like, have been excluded from the glossary as these would be familiar to most readers. So too are excluded those words whose meaning is clear from the context.

Benjamin WALKER's *Hindu World* (Allen & Unwin, London, 1968) and John DOWSON's *Dictionary of Hindu Mythology* (Routledge, London, 1961) have been of great help in preparing the glossary and their assistance is gratefully acknowledged.

A NOTE ON RHYME

It is impossible to convey in translation the rhythmic lilt of Hindi poetry. This is why the transliterated version of the Hindi text is given along with the English one. The use of rhymes, especially end-rhymes, is a distinctive feature of Hindi poetry. This is apparent from a number of verses of *Rāmacandrikā*, as for example:

Ati ucca agārani banī pagārani janu cintāmaṇi nāri.
Bahu śata makha-dhūmani-dhūpita aṅgana Hari kī sī anuhāri.
Citrī bahu citrani parama vicitrana Keśavadāsa nihāri.
Janu viśvarūpa ko amala ārasī racī birañci bicāri.

The City of Ajōdhyā, Ch. 1,v. 45

Note the end-rhymes (*nāri*, *anuhāri*, *nihāri*, *bicāri*) as well as the rhymes in (*agārani*, *pagārani*) (*Bahu śata makha-dhūmani-dhūpita aṅgana*) and (*Citrī bahu citrani parama vicitrana*).

The second marked characteristic of Hindi verse is the use of alliteration. This is apparent from a number of verses in the book. As an example the following verse may be taken:

Phūle palāsa vilāsa thalī bahu Keśavadāsa prakāśan a thore.
Śeśa aśeṣa mukhānal kī janu jvāl vishāl chalī divi ore.
Kimshuk Shrī shuktuṇḍan kī *ruchi rāche rasātal chit chore.*
Choṁchan chāṁpi chahūṁdis ḍolat *cāru cakor* agāran bhore.

From *Spring*, Ch. 30, v. 35

The alliterations in the above verse are italicised.

Another feature is the use of onomatopoeic words. It is this which gives Hindi poetry its distinctive melody, a quality which is, alas, lost in translation. In the description of dawn in Chapter 30 the gradual rising of the sun, the disappearance of the planets and of the stars one by one in the bright sun's light, the flying away of swarms of restless black bees from the lovely and delicate lotuses, and the fading of the lamplight in the sun's brightness, is aptly described in soft sounding words expressing forcefully the gentle coming of dawn:

Jāgiye trilokdeva, *devadeva Rāmadeva,*
Bhor bhayo bhūmideva bhakta daras pāvaiṁ.
Brahmā man mantrabarṇa Bishnuhṛdaya-cātak ghan,
Rudrahṛdaya-kamal-mitra, jagatgīta gāvaiṁ.
Gagan udit Ravi ananta, shukrādik jyotivant,
Chhan chhan chhabi chhīn hot, līn pīn tāre.
Mānahu pardeśa deśa, Brahmadosh ke praveś,
Ṭhaur ṭhaur te vilāt jāt bhūp bhāre.

From *Dawn*, Ch. 30 v.18

The words *devadeva Rāmadeva*, *Bhor bhayo bhūmideva*, and *chhan chhan chhabi chhīn hot*, are particularly expressive.

The only way in which the rich melody of Hindi verse can be appreciated by an English reader is by reading it in the transliterated version with the help of diacritical marks. It is hoped that its inclusion will preserve this valuable trait of Hindi poetry which would be completely lost if only the translation of the text was given.

Sarjū (From Chapter 1)

On his visit to Ajodhyā, sage Viśvāmitra[1] *and his friends go round the city, and then move along the banks of the Sarjū river.*[2] *The lines which follow describe the thoughts which come to the saint's mind on seeing the river.*

26-27. Ati nipaṭ kuṭil gati yadapi āp.
Tau datt shuddha gati chhuvat āp.
Kachhu apun adh adhgati chalanti.
Phal patitan kaṁh ūradh phalanti.

1. A famous sage who was born a Kṣatriya, but by rigorous austerities raised himself to the Brahmin caste, and became one of the seven *ṛṣis*. According to the *Ṛgveda* he was the son of King Kuśika, but other authorities consider him to be the son of Gādhi, a descendant of Puru. Viśvāmitra had a long quarrel with sage Vasiṣṭha, which was finally patched up. The *Mahābhārata* and *Rāmāyaṇa* tell the story of Viśvāmitra's amour with Menakā who was deliberately sent by Indra to seduce him. She succeeded, and gave birth to Śakuntalā. The sage had another love affair with the nymph Rambhā.

In the *Rāmāyaṇa* we hear a lot about Viśvāmitra. It was he who prevailed upon King Daśaratha to send his son, Rāma, for the protection of the Brahmins against the attack of the demons. The sage acted as his *guru*, and returned to Ayodhyā with Rāma, where the prince obtained the hand of Sītā.

Here Viśvāmitra is going to Ayodhyā for the first time, to request King Daśaratha to spare his son, Rāma, for the task of killing the demons.

2. A tributary of the River Gaṅgā on which the sacred city of Ayodhyā lies. An account of the Sarajū river given in the *Fyzabad Gazetteer* is as follows :—'During the rains the river attains an immense size and volume. It is extraordinarily erratic in its action, and frequently changes its channel from year to year, shifting from side to side of its wide sandy bed. In the cold weather, and during the early summer months, the river shrinks to comparatively small dimensions; it leaves on either side a broad stretch of rich alluvial land, although in places there are wide expanses of sand covered by tamarisk jungle. The river is considered sacred by the Hindus. (*Fyzabad*, *A gazetteer*, H.R. *NEVILL*, I.C.S., Allahabad, 1905). Of the Sarajū river, Tulasīdāsa says in the *Rāmāyaṇa* : 'The *Vedas* and *Purāṇas* say that the very sight, touch, and taste of the Sarajū river, washes away sins. This river is very holy. Its grandeur is eternal, of which even Sarasvatī of stainless wisdom can't relate'. *Rāmāyaṇa*, *Bālakāṇḍa* 34.1).

Mad matt yadapi mātang sang.
Ati tadapi patit pāvan terang.
Bahu nhāye nhāya jehi saneh.
Sab jāt svarg sūkar jal sadeh.

What Saint Viśvāmitra said to the River

Although you flow
twisting and turning,
you make others straight
by the mere touch
of your water.
You flow downward,
but raise to heaven
fallen sinners.[3]

Though intoxicated elephants
wash themselves in you,
your waves purify
evil men.

Many living creatures
bathe joyfully
in you;

3. The Gaṅgā and its tributaries are considered holy, and the Hindus believe that bathing in their waters washes away all sins. The Gaṅgā is believed to flow from the toe of Lord Viṣṇu. It was brought down from heaven by the penance of sage Bhagīratha—hence called Bhāgīrathī. To save the earth from the sudden force of its torrent as it fell from heaven, the god Śiva caught it in his matted locks. Many of India's holy cities and centres of pilgrimages are on the banks of the Gaṅgā, e.g., Hardwar, Rishikesh, Gaḍhamukteshwar, Varanasi, and Allahabad (Prayag).

When a Hindu dies, his relations cremate him, if possible, at one of the ghats along this holy river. Any person bathing in the river acquires merit, and being freed from all sin goes to heaven. The *Purāṇas* relate how a bone of a dead dog, while being carried over the Gaṅgā by a crow, was accidentally dropped into the holy waters, as a result of which the dog was instantly translated to heaven.

and all of them,
even the miserable pig,
go bodily
to heaven.

Godāvarī (From Chapter 11)

Rāma and Lakṣmaṇa have built a hut of leaves by the Godāvarī river and have made it their temporary home. The river Godāvarī which enters into the Bay of Bengal on the eastern coast of India is a large perennial river. In his description Keśavadāsa follows his usual pattern of deifying the river and praising its purifying qualities. The description closely follows the one of the river Sarjū.

Rāma :

23. Ati nikaṭ Godāvarī pāp sanhāriṇī.
Cal tarang tungāvalī cāru sañcāriṇī.
Ali kamal saugandh līlā manohāriṇī.
Bahu nayan devesha-shobhā mano dhāriṇī.

What Rāma said :

Near my hut flows
the sin-destroying Godāvarī,
with waves
high, tempestuous, and majestic:
the perfumed lotuses in it
round which blackbees hover
are like the numerous eyes
of god Indra,[4]
and captivate
the soul.

4. Indra is god of the firmament. He is described as being of a ruddy complexion, having arms of enormous length. His forms are endless, and he can assume any shape at will.

24. Rīti mano aviveka kī thāpī,
Sādhun kī gati pāvat pāpī.
Kanjan kī mati sī baṛabhāgi.
Śrī Hari mandir soṁ anurāgī.

Even if a sinner
bathes in the Godāvarī
he goes to heaven.

As Brahmā's mind
is forever fixed on paradise,
so the Godāvarī
keeps flowing
towards the sea.

25. Nipaṭ pativrat dharaṇī
Magjan ko sukhkaraṇī
Nigati sadā gati sunie
Agati mahāpati gunie.

The sea is like
Godāvarī's husband:
she is always
faithful to him:
yet she pleases
all those men
who come to her.

He rides in a bright golden car, drawn by tawny or ruddy horses with flowing manes and tails. His weapon is the thunderbolt, which he carried in his right hand; he also uses arrows, a great hook, and a net, in which he is said to entangle his foes. The *soma* juice (wine) is his special delight and he takes enormous draughts of it. As deity of the atmosphere he governs the weather and dispenses the rain. According to the *Mahābhārata* he seduced, or endeavoured to seduce, Ahalyā, the wife of sage Gautama, and that sage's curse impressed upon him a thousand marks resembling the female organ. But these marks were afterwards changed to eyes, and hence he is called Netrayoni (*netra* =eyes; *yoni*=the female organ) or Sahasrākṣa, the thousand-eyed (*sahasra*=one thousand; *akṣi*= eye).

She carries sinners
swiftly heaven's way,
yet keeps the sea
    stagnant.

26. Bishmaya bah Godāvarī, amrit ke phal deti
Keśav jīvanhār ko, dukkha aśeṣa hari leti.

This brimful river
gives immortality
to all who bathe in it:
says Keśavadāsa
it destroys
the grief of those who drink
its water.

Triveṇī (From Chapter 20)

The long war between the armies of Rāma and Rāvaṇa was at last over and Sītā was freed from her confinement at Laṅkā. Her ordeals, however, were not ended. Rāma had to prove to his followers that Sītā was unsullied by sin during her long abode in Laṅkā, so he caused a fire to be lit, and Sītā entered into it. But the fire could not even touch such a pure woman, and at Brahmā's command the god of fire lifted her from it and restored her to Rāma. Then Rāma asked god Indra to revive all the monkeys who had been slain in the battle. When they were risen from the dead they mounted the celestial car, and Rāma, Lakṣmaṇa, and Sītā, departed for Ayodhyā. On the way they visited Prayāg the holy city on the confluence of the Gaṅgā and Yamunā, where flowed the sacred Sarasvatī and paid their respects to sage Bharadvāja. Here poet Keśavadāsa gives a description of the Triveṇī—'the triple braid', so called because the rivers Gaṅgā and Yamunā unite here, and the Sarasvatī is believed to join them by an underground channel.

29. Chilke duti sūchham śobhati bārū.
Tanu 'hvai janu sovat haiṁ sur chārū.

Pratibimbit dip dipeṁ jal māhīṁ.
Janu jvālmukhīn ke jāl nahāhīṁ.

The grains of fine sand
shine as though
heavenly gods
with tiny bodies
were serving Triveṇī.

The flames
of the lighted lamps
reflected in the water,
seem like many goddesses
bathing.

30. Jal kī duti pīt sitāsit sohai.
ati pātak ghāt karai jag ko hai.
Madeṇa malai ghasi kumkum nīko.
Nrip Bhāratkhaṇḍ diyo janu ṭīko.

The water of the river
which destroys
all grievous sins
glimmers
white,
yellow, and
black.

The Triveṇī looks
like Bhāratkhaṇḍ[5]

5. Bhāratakhaṇḍa literally means the land of Bhārata i.e. India, but here it is used for some king who is resplendent with *ṭikā* mark of black musk, white sandal-paste, and yellow saffron, all rubbed together. A *ṭikā* mark is a sacerdotal or an ornamental mark made on the forehead, of various shapes. King Bhāratakhaṇḍa can mean either (i) a king whose descendants were a warlike people called Bharatas (frequently mentioned in the *Ṛgveda*, or (ii) an ancient king of the first *Manvantara*, devoted to Viṣṇu, who was born as a deer because he took compassion on a newly born deer, and after many births obtained emancipation or (iii) a prince of the Puru branch of the lunar race, son of Duṣyanta and Śakuntalā. Most probably the king meant here is the ancestor of the warlike Bharatas.

with a *ṭīkā* mark
on his forehead
of a paste of
sandal-wood
saffron, and
musk.

31. Chatur badan panchbadan shaṭbadan,
Sahas badan hūṁ sahas gati gāī hai
Sāt lok sāt dvīp sātahū rasātalan,
Gaṅgā jī kī shobhā sabahīṁ ko sukhadāī hai.
Jamunā ko jal raho phaili ke pravāh par,
Keshodāsa bīch bīch Giri kī gorāī haī.
Shobhan sharīra par kumkum bilepan kai,
Shyāmal dukūl jhīn jhankat jhāmi hai.

Brahmā, Śiva, Kārttikeya,[6]
and Śeṣa,[7]
have in a thousand ways
sung its praises:
in the seven
worlds,
dvīpas, and
nether worlds,[8]

6. The god of war and of the planet Mars, also called Skanda. He was born without the intervention of a woman. Śiva cast his seed into the fire, and it was afterwards received by the Gaṅgā, and so gave birth to Kārttikeya. Some believe the Gaṅgā, Agni (fire), or Pārvatī to be his mother. He has ten heads and rides a peacock, holding a bow in one hand and an arrow in the other. His wife is Kumārī or Senā.

7. King of the serpents or *nāgas*, and of the infernal regions called Pātāla. A serpent with a thousand heads which is the couch and canopy of Viṣṇu whilst sleeping during the intervals of creation. Sometimes he is shown supporting the world and sometimes upholding the seven *pātālas* or hells. Whenever he yawns he causes earthquakes. At the end of each *Kalpa* he vomits venomous fire which destroys all creation. When the gods churned the ocean they made use of Śeṣa as a great rope which they twisted round the mount Mandara and used it as a churn. He is represented as clothed in purple, wearing a white necklace, holding in one hand a plough, and in the other a pestle. He is also known as *Ananta*, 'the endless', as a symbol of eternity.

8. Three worlds (see note 152), are the three *dvīpas* —a *dvīpa* is an insular continent. The *dvīpas* stretch out from the mountain Meru as

Gaṇgā's splendour
gives pleasure.
The Jamunā joins it,
and, says Keśava, between them
the white Sarasvatī
is like a lovely woman
whose body
anointed with saffron
shines from beneath
a thin black sari.

Sugriva:

32. Bhavsāgar kī janu setu ujāgar sundartā sigarī bas kī.
Tihuṁ devan kī duti sī darsai gati sokhai tridoshan ke ras kī.
Kahi Keshav Vedatrayī mati sī paritāptrayī tal ko masakī.
Sab badaiṁ trikāl triloka Tribeṇihiṁ ketu tribikrama ke jas kī.

What Sugrīva said

The Triveṇī
is like a bridge
over the ocean
of worldly existence:
it has brought all splendour
under its sway,

their common centre, like the leaves of a lotus, and are separated from each other by distinct circumambient oceans. They are said to be seven in number—Jambū, Plakṣa, Śālmala, Kuśa, Krauñca, Śāka, and Puṣkara; and the seas which surround them are—Lavaṇa (salt water), Ikṣu (sugar-cane juice), Surā (wine), Sarpis or Ghṛta (clarified butter), Dadhi (curd), Dugdha or Kṣīra (milk), and Jala (fresh water). In the *Mahābhārata*, however, only four *dvīpas* are known, while the *Viṣṇu Purāṇa* divides India into nine *dvīpas* or portions.

The seven nether worlds are the *pātālas*. These are inhabited by *nāgas* (serpents), *daityas* and *dānavas* (demons), *yakṣas* (demigods) and others. They are seven according to *Viṣṇu Purāṇa*, viz. Atala, Vitala, Nitala, Gabhastimat, Mahātala, Sutala, and Pātāla. The *Śiva Purāṇa*, however, mentions eight. The sage Nārada, who paid a visit to these regions, declared them to be far more delightful than Indra's heaven, and abounding with every kind of luxury and sensual gratification.

and shines with the light
of the three gods.[9]

It cures men
of the three diseases[10]
caused by wind, bile, and phlegm,
and saves them from death.

Says Keśavadāsa,
the Triveṇī is pure
as the three Vedas:
it drives the three sins
to the nether regions.

The people of all the three worlds
pay homage to it
in all the three ages,[11]
because it is the banner
of famed Vāman.[12]

Vibhīṣaṇa

33. Bhūtal kī beṇī sī Triveṇī subh shobijati,
Ek kahaiṁ surpur mārag bibhāt hai.

9. The three gods are those of the Hindu *trimūrti*—Brahmā the Creator, Viṣṇu the Preserver, and Śiva the Destroyer. The light of Brahmā is yellowish—the colour of the Sarasvatī river, the light of Viṣṇu is darkish—the colour of the river Yamunā whose waters are considered black (due to its depth), the light of Śiva is whitish—the colour of the river Gaṅgā.

10. The three diseases are those which are physical like illness and the like, the ones of divine origin, and the mundane troubles which living in the world involves.

11. The three ages are the past, present and the future.

12. Vāmana='the dwarf'. King Bali, the demon king, had by his devotions and austerities acquired the dominion of the three worlds, and the gods lost dignity. To set this right, Viṣṇu was born as a diminutive son of Kaśyapa and Aditi. The dwarf asked a boon of Bali, and on being granted it, stepped over both heaven and earth, but out of consideration for the King left him to rule over Pātāla, the infernal regions. Thus Vāmana is an *avatāra* or incarnation of Viṣṇu (see also note 172).

Ekai kahaiṁ pūraṇa anādi jo ananta kou,
Tāko yah Keśavadāsa dravarūp gāt hai.
Sab sukhkar sab shobhākar mere jān,
Kauno yah adbhut sugandhi avadāt hai.
Daras paras hī te thir char jīvan kī,
Koṭi koṭi janmā ki kugandhi miṭi jāt hai.

What Vibhīṣaṇa said

The Triveṇi is charming
as the peak of the earth,
it is like a road
to heaven;
or the watery form
of the eternal Lord.
It is the source
of all splendour
and bliss.

It seems to me
a wonderfully chaste
and perfumed object,
which by the mere touch
washes off countless sins
of creatures still and moving.

King Daśaratha's Garden (From Chapter 1)

The description of Daśaratha's garden is given by Keśavadāsa through sage Viśvāmitra. After visiting the river Sarjū and seeing the elephants in the King's palace, the sage enjoys the beauty of the garden, and the description which follows is in his words.

30. Dekhi bāg anurāg upajjiye.
Bolat kal dhvani kokil sajjiye.
Rājati rati kī sakhī subeshani.
Manahuṁ bahati manmath saṁdeshani.

The bower
is captivating;
the cuckoo singing in it
melodiously
seems like Rati's[13] companion,
proclaiming the message
of God's
love.

31. Phūli phūli taru phūl baṛhāvat.
Modat mahāmod upajāvat.
Uṛat parāg na chitta uṛāvat.
Bhramar bhramat nahiṁ jīva bhramāvat.

The strollers in the garden
are delighted
to see the blossoms
covering the trees,
and their hearts
are gladdened
with their perfume.

The pollen
flying in the air
is as though men's minds
soaring.

The murmuring black bees
seem to be human souls
which, taking their shape,
wander about.

32-33. Subh sar shobhai
Muni man lobhai.
Sarsij phūle.
Ali ras bhūle

13. Rati, the Venus of the Hindus, meaning 'love' or 'desire', is the name of the wife of Kāmadeva, the Hindu god of love. She is the daughter of Dakṣa and is famed for her great beauty.

Black Berries (By Bireswar Sen)

[to face p. 45

Jal char ḍolaiṁ
Bahu khag bolaiṁ
Baraṇi na jāhiṁ
Ḍar urjhāhiṁ.

In the midst of the bower
there's a pond so lovely
that it charms
even sages.
Lotuses bloom in it,
and black bees
drunk with their nectar,
Swarm round them.

The fishes sporting
in the pond,
and many water-birds
warbling:
defy description,
and captivate
the soul.

34. Dekh[illegible] banvārī chanchal bhārī tadapi tapodhan mānī.
Ati [illegible]pmai lekhī grahathit pekhī jagat digambar jānī
Jag yadapi digambar pushpavatī nar nirakhi nirakhi man mohai.
Puni pushpavatī tan ati ati pāvan garbha sahit sab sohai.

(1)

The garden
with its leaves and flowers
swaying in the breeze
seems like a forest girl,
and it braves the cold,
sun, and rain,
as a woman engaged in austerities.

Though 'tis as a wandering hermit
it is confined

within boundary walls:
though chaste
and hid from men's eyes,
its beautiful flowers
can be seen by everyone.
The small fruits
inside the blossoms
on the trees
are very attractive.

Or

(2)

This forest girl
is restless,
yet calm as a woman
engaged in austerity.
Though an ascetic
she remains at home:
though a grown up girl
she goes about naked:
though desireless
she lusts after men:
and though in her menses
she's pure, and
pregnant.[14]

35. Puni garbh saṁyogī ratirasa bhogī jag jan līn kahāvai.
Guni jagjan līnā nagar pravīnā ati pati ke man bahāvai.
Ati patihi ramāvai citta bhramāvai sautin prem baṛhāvai.
Abyau dinrātin adbhut bhātin kavikul kīrati gāvai.

(1)

To this garden
full of fruit trees
come

14. In this verse the word *banavārī* has been given a double meaning —(i) A flower-garden, and (ii) a maiden living in the forest—in order to produce an effect of contrariness or contrast. The meaning, taking the word in the sense of a flower-garden, is the one intended, and the literal one, while the other is merely for the sake of embellishment by introducing oxymoron. The former is given in the text. If the word *banavārī* is taken to mean a forest-maiden the sense would be as in the alternative verse.

The same double-meaning is continued in the next verse.

admirers,
wise men of the world,
and clever citizens.

The garden
excites King Daśaratha's[15]
passion,
so that he makes love
to all his co-wives;[16]
therefore they too
love it,
and come there often
with the King.
Many poets
lavish their praises
on this wonderful
garden.

Or

(2)

Though pregnant
the forest girl
makes love to other men,
and yet remains
her husband's
beloved.

15. Son of Aja, a descendant of Ikṣvāku, and a prince of the solar race, Daśaratha was the father of Rāma the hero of the *Rāmāyaṇa*. He had three wives, Kauśalyā, Kaikeyī and Sumitrā. It is said that Lord Viṣṇu promised the gods to become incarnate as man for the destruction of Rāvaṇa—the ten-headed demon king. He chose Daśaratha for his human parent. When Daśaratha (King of Ayodhyā) was performing a sacrifice for obtaining progeny he came out of the fire as a glorious being and gave him a vessel full of nectar to administer to his wives. As a result they became pregnant and bore sons—Kauśalyā giving birth to Rāma, Kaikeyī to Bharata, and Sumitrā to Lakṣmaṇa and Śatrughna.

16. Co-wives were rival wives. Vātsyāyana advocates harmony between rival wives in *Kāma-Sūtra*—'When the second wife is married, and brought into the house, the first wife should give her a position superior to her own, and look upon her as a sister'. (*Kāma-Sūtra*, Luxor Press, London). In practice however there was much jealousy, rivalry and bitterness between co-wives.

Though she is
her husband's favourite,
her co-wives love her
even more
because of it.

The Pañcavaṭī Forest (From Chapter 11)

The description of the Pañcavaṭī forest occurs in the eleventh chapter of the book. Owing to the machination of Mantharā, the humpbacked nurse of Kaikeyī, (one of the queens of King Daśaratha), Rāma was banished from his kingdom to reside in the forest for fourteen years. His faithful wife, Sītā, and brother, Lakṣmaṇa, went with him. Crossing the River Jamunā they came to the Chitrakūṭ mountain where they built a hut by the river Mandākinī and lived for some days. Thereafter wandering through the lonely forest, slaying demons, and relieving the grief-stricken, they arrived, ten years after leaving Ayodhyā, at the hermitage of the sage Agastya. The sage advised them to go to Pañcavaṭī by the bank of the river Godāvarī. Soon they came to a place where five great banyan trees grew—this was Pañcavaṭī (pañca = five). It was a lovely spot in the midst of the desolate forest, full of bright flowers on which gay bees hummed seeking nectar, and many kinds of coloured birds which warbled sweetly. Here the weary travellers rested and made it their abode.

In the following verses Keśavadāsa describes the beauty of the Pañcavaṭī forest.

17. Phal phūlan pūre, taruvar rūre, kokil kul kalrav bolaiṁ.
Ati matta mayūri, piya rasa pūri, ban-ban prati nācat dolaiṁ.
Sārī śuk paṇḍit, gun gan maṇḍit, bhāvanāmaya arath bakhānaiṁ.
Dekh Raghunāyak, Sīya sahāyak, manahu Madan Rati madhujānaiṁ.

As soon as Rāma entered the forest
flowers and fruit

suddenly appeared
on the bare branches.

The cuckoos sang
in a soft melodious voice :
the peahens wandered about
filled with longing
for copulation.

The parrots and starlings
began to describe
like learned pundits
the beauty of their dance
and song.

Seeing Rāma, Sītā, and Lakṣhmaṇa
the creatures of the forest
took them to be Kāmadeva
along with Ratī
and Basant.[17]

Lakṣmaṇa :

18. Sab jāti phaṭī dukh kī dupaṭī kapaṭī na rahai jahṁ ek ghaṭī.
Nighaṭī ruchi mīchu ghaṭī hūṁ ghaṭī jagjīva jatīn kī chhaṭī taṭī.
Agh ogh kī berā kaṭī vikaṭī nikaṭī pragaṭī guru jñāna gaṭī.
Chahuṁ oran nāchati mukti naṭī gun ghūrjaṭī ban Pañchavaṭī.

What Lakṣmaṇa said

As god Shiva
destroys all sorrows
so this Pañchavaṭī forest
removes grief.

17. *Basant* (or *Vasanta*) is the Indian spring season and its deified personification. It is associated with the god of love (Kāmadeva) and his wife Rati, here, because spring is the season for love.

It makes the deceitful man
turn towards *dharma*[18]
and gives such great bliss
to those who live in it
that they have no desire
for *moksha*[19] or *samādhi*.[20]

Sin is driven away
and illumination attained
in a moment.
In this forest
Salvation dances
all around
as a dancing
woman.

The Daṇḍaka Forest (From Chapter 11)

The forest of Pañchavaṭī described in the previous verses, was a portion of the Daṇḍaka forest. There was a king of the name of Daṇḍaka whose preceptor was Śukrāchārya. The king looked on the sage's daughter with evil intent, as a result of which Śukrāchārya

18. Religious and moral duty, the path of right action. *Dharma* comes from *dhṛ*='to hold,' or 'to support'. It means 'prop', 'support', or 'law'. Later it came to mean 'customary law', 'religious injunction', or 'duty'—that which supports the universe as well as society. *Dharma* governs a man's attitude towards the external world and his mental and physical reaction in any given situation. It is what a man should do to keep his moral conduct above reproach.

19. Emancipation. Hindus believe that man is reborn in the world according to his past actions. This cycle of rebirth is broken only when knowledge of the Absolute (*Brahman*, not to be confused with Brahmin=priestly class) is attained. In this state of emancipation (*mokṣa*), which is one of unspeakable bliss, the liberated soul becomes one with the Absolute and does not have to suffer rebirth. *Mokṣa* is the state of the greatest bliss.

20. *Samādhi*, is transcendental contemplation or ecstasy—a supernormal state produced by meditation, concentration, etc. It is the eighth step of Patañjali's *Yoga* system, the others being (i) Self-control (*yama*), (ii) Religious duty (*niyama*), (iii) Postures (*āsana*), (iv) Control of breath (*prāṇāyāma*), (v) Control of the senses (*pratyāhāra*), (vi) Control of the mind (*dhāraṇā*), and (vii) Meditation (*dhyāna*).

caused hot sand to rain on his kingdom for seven days and seven nights, and laid waste the land. The same kingdom came to be known as Daṇḍaka. When Rāma entered this spot it became verdant again and the trees turned green and full of flowers and fruits. Keśavadāsa gives an account of this transformation in the verses following.

19. Śobhat Daṇḍak kī rucī banī,
Bhāṁtin-bhāṁtin sundar ghanī.
Sevā baṛe nrip kī janu lasai,
Śrīphal bhūri bhayo jahaṁ basai.

With Rāma's coming
the splendour
of the Daṇḍaka forest
revived :
the wood apple grew
profusely in it,
as wealth increases
when a king
serves his country
well.

20. Ber bhayānak sī ati lagai,
Ark samūh jahāṁ jag magai.
Nainan ko bahu rūpan grasai,
Shrī Harī kī janu mūrat lasai.

The flowering coral clusters
sparkle as the blaze
of many suns
in *pralaya*.[21]

The splendour
of the Daṇḍaka forest
is like that of Hari's image[22]
on which the eyes
never tire
of gazing.

21. The dissolution of the world at the end of a *kalpa*, a *kalpa* being a day and a night of Brahmā i.e. 8,640,000,000 years.
22. Hari means Viṣṇu—the Preserver (see note 162).

21. Pāṇḍava kī pratimā sam leko.
Arjuna Bhīma mahāmati dekho.
Hai subhagā sam dīpati pūrī
Siṁdūr aur tilkāvali rūrī.

What Rāma said

Wise Lakṣmaṇa,
the forest here
is like the image
of the Pāṇḍavas.[23]

The *kukubha* tree stands
as proud Arjuna,
and the sorrel
as sturdy Bhīma.

The line of oak
and *tilak*[24] trees,
are splendid as a woman
adorned with vermilion
and *ṭikā* marks.[25]

23. The five sons of Pāṇḍu who fought with the Kauravas in the Mahābhārata—'the great war of the Bharatas'. These were Yudhiṣṭhira (firm in fight) *yuddha*=fight, *sthira*=firm, Bhīma (the terrible) noted for his strength, Arjuna (the bright or silvery) brave, high-minded and generous. Nakula and Sahadeva, both of whom were spirited and amiable. They had vowed to share all things in common, and so married a common wife—Draupadī, the lovely daughter of Drupada, King of the Pañcālas.

24. *Tilaka* is a tree of the nutmeg variety. It means both such a tree, or an ornamental decorative mark on the forehead made by women. In this verse there are four words having double meanings. *Arjuna* means either the Pāṇḍava warrior, or the tree known by this name (also called *kukubha* or *kukuca*). *Bhīma* means the Pāṇḍava warrior of this name or the *bhīma* tree (a type of sorrel). *Sindūra* is (i) vermilion, or (ii) the Sindūra or oak tree. Lastly *tilaka* means either (i) a forest tree of the type of nutmeg or (ii) a decorative mark made on the forehead by women.

25. Hindu women adorned their foreheads and cheeks by round *ṭikā* marks made by coloured pastes or powders or vermilion. Sometimes bright metal discs were used which they stuck on the cheeks or forehead to form a lovely pattern.

Sītā :

22. Rājati hai yah jyoṁ kulkanyā
Dhāī birājit hai sag dhanyā.
Kelithalī janu Śrī Girijā kī.
Śobh dhare sitkaṇṭh prabhā kī.

What Sītā said

The forest's splendour
is like that of a girl
of noble family :
and in it the *dhavāi* tree[26]
is as a wet nurse
for her children.

The forest's splendour
is like a spot
for Pārvatī's[27] dalliance :
and as Śaṅkar
is always there,
so does the peacock
frequent it.

Lake Pampā (From Chapter 12)

While residing in Pañcavaṭī in the Daṇḍaka forest a number of events took place which brought misfortune to Rāma. Śūrpaṇakhā, the widowed sister of Rāvaṇa the demon king, fell in love with him and wanted to marry him. Rāma suggested Lakṣmaṇa to her as a match and Lakṣmaṇa sent her back to Rāma. This enraged Śūrpaṇakhā, and she began to frighten Sītā. Lakṣmaṇa thereupon cut off her nose. Her brother, Rāvaṇa, determined to avenge this insult, and with the aid of the demon, Mārīca, managed to abduct Sītā. Rāma, and

26. The word *dhāi* has a double meaning here. It stands for (i) a wet-nurse. Women of high-caste families engaged such nurses for their children, and also as companions. (ii) A forest tree called *dhavāi*, *dhava*, or *dhāvā*.

27. Wife of Śiva—the Destroyer, (See note 128).

his brother, were grief-stricken at Sītā's disappearance and began to wander, sorrowfully in the forest in her search. After some adventures they made for the Ṛṣyamūk mountains. On the way they came across the Pampā river and the pond of that name. Here there were innumerable birds of bright plumage, deer sporting in pairs, milk-white swans gliding on the waters of the lake, and gay butterflies lazying about. It is this lake which poet Keśavadāsa now describes.

47. Ati sundar sītal som basai,
Jahṁ rūpa anekani lobh lasai.
Bahu paṅkaj pakṣi virājat haiṁ,
Raghunāth vilokat lājat haiṁ.

The Pampā lake
is so cool and beautiful
that even great hermits
are tempted to stay there
for ever :
many kinds of lotuses and birds
are there, but they cannot match
Rāma's beauty.[28]

48. Sigarī ritu sobhi shubhra jahīṁ,
Lah grīsham pāi na pravesh sahī.
Nava nīraj nīr tahāṁ sarasaiṁ,
Siyā ke subh lochan se darasaiṁ.

All seasons are there
but summer afflicts not :
young lotuses are blossoming,
which appear
as Sītā's lovely eyes.[29]

28. The beauty of Rāma eclipses that of the lotus and the birds, and it is because of this reason that they feel ashamed.

29. In Sanskrit and Hindi literature the favourite symbol for beautiful eyes is the lotus. Śakuntalā's eyes are like lotuses. Bhartṛhari, in his *Śatakas*, praises eyes 'that surpass the beauty of the lotus'. Bāṇa describes the eyes of the companion of Mālatī as 'a string of blue lotus petals'. In *The Toycart*, Vasantasenā, the courtesan, had eyes which put to shame the seeds of the red lotus. In *Daśakumāracarita* the eyes of sleeping princesses are describd as 'two inverted blue lotuses.' In the *Mahābhārata*, Draupadi

49. Sundar set saroruha meṁ karhāṭak hāṭak kī duti ko hai.
Tāpar bhauṁr bhalo manrochan lok bilochan kī ruchiro hai.
Dekhi deī upamā jaladebin dīragh devan ke man mohai.
Keshav Keshavrāye mano Kamalāsan ke sir ūpar sohai.

The yellowish stamen
of the lovely white lotus
looks like a yellow umbrella
and onlookers are charmed
by the beautiful black bee
sitting on it.
The river goddesses
describe this sight
in words which captivate
the minds of gods
even,
the black bee upon the yellow umbrella,
they say
is as Viṣṇu sitting
on Brahmā's head.[30]

is described as having eyes 'like the leaves of the autumn lotus'. Priyadarśikā, the beloved of King Harṣa, had lotus eyes, and the heroine of Bihāri's *Love Poems* had dust-like eyes 'of three colours which shamed the lotus flower'. The comparison of Sītā's eyes to lotuses here, therefore, follows the literary tradition.

30. Keśavadāsa has given a quaint simile here in comparing the lotus with the yellow umbrella on which the black bee is sitting, to Viṣṇu sitting on Brahmā. However, the reason for giving the simile is that firstly Brahmā is said to be of a red colour (see note 124), and the petals of the lotus are either white or of a light reddish colour. Secondly Viṣṇu (see note 162) is said to be of a dark blue colour which would approximate to the colour of the black bee. Besides Viṣṇu is sometimes represented as seated on a lotus along with his consort, Lakṣmī, or reclining on a leaf of that plant. Hence the imagery of Viṣṇu seated on the Brahmā-like lotus would be in keeping with such a representation.

The Pond (From Chapter 32).

Rāma and his friend Shuk were peeping at the beautiful maid-servants of Sītā. Suddenly the women saw them and were abashed. Sītā, laughed and asked Rāma to show her the garden. Rāma took her and her companions, to the newly planted garden. There they admired the beauty of the trees and flowers and saw the rockery which Rāma had got made and the three artificial streams flowing from it. When he saw that Sītā, was tired, Rāma turned towards the pond which was nearby, and along with Sītā, rested on its bank. In the verses which follow, poet Keśavadāsa describes the beauty of the pond.

33. Āī kamal-bāsu sukhdain.
Mukh-bāsan āge 'hvai lain
Dekhyo jāya jalāshaya chāru
Shītal sukhad sugandha apāru.

From far away
the refreshing scent
of lotuses came,
as though to greet
the sweet perfume
of the women's mouths :
and soon they saw
a big, cool, pleasing, fragrant,
and lovely,
pond.

34. Banshrī ko darpanu, chandrātap janu, kidhauṁ sharad āvās.
Muni jan gan man so virahī jan so, bis balayāni bilās.
Pratibimbit thirchar, jīva manohar, manu Hari udar ananta.
Bandhanyut sohai, Tribhuvan mohai, māno Bali jasvant.

This pond
is a mirror
to reflect
the garden's beauty

or perhaps
the moonlight
itself.

Or a house for Autumn
to live in.
It is unsullied
as the minds of sages
and as a lover in separation
it bears on itself
lotuses,
roots,
and the like.[31]

Creatures still and living
are reflected
in its clear water :
it is like
the endless abdomen
of Viṣṇu,[32]
and get renown
in all the three worlds[33]
by being bound by its ghats,
as King Bali got
by his bondage.

35. Vishamaya pai sukh ko dhām.
Shambar rūpa baṛhāvai kāma.
Kamalan madhya bhramar sukh det.
Sant hridaya janu Harihi samet.

This pond full of water
is deadly,[34]

31. Lovers who are separated hold near their bodies lotuses, cool roots, and other cooling things, in order to lessen the heat of their ardour.

32. The whole world is supposed to be contained in Hari's (Viṣṇu's) abdomen.

33. Bali was the Daitya king whom Vāmana—the dwarf *avatāra* (incarnation) of Viṣṇu—bound with his prayer of obtaining three vows. (See note 12).

34. There is a pun on the word *viṣamaya*. It means (i) full of water, i.e., the lake is full of water or (ii) full of poison.

and yet pleasing :
It is fierce
like the demon, Shambar,[35]
but 'tis not Kāmadeva's enemy :
on the contrary
it increases
passion.

The black bees hovering
between the lotuses
are charming ;
as though Viṣṇu
was himself enshrined
in the minds
of sages.

36. Bīch bīch sohaiṁ jaljāt.
Jitate alikul uṛi uṛi jāt.
Sant hiyan teṁ mānahu bhāji.
Chanchal chalā ashub kī rāji.

The black bees
flying off occasionally
from single lotuses
in between lotus clusters,
seem like evil desires
escaping
from the minds
of sages.

35. Śambara was a demon who abducted Rati, wife, of Kāma, god of love, and so became his foe. The poet says the pond is of the form of the demon, Śambara, but instead of being Kāma's foe, he increases *Kāma* (i.e. passion).

Chastisement of the Sea by Rāmachandra
(By Raja Ravi Verma)

[to face p. 59

The Sea (From Chapter 14)

Having formed an alliance with Sugrīva, the ape-king and Hanumān, the monkey-god, Rāma made preparations for invading Laṅkā, the kingdom of Rāvaṇa, the ten-headed demon-king who had carried away Sītā. Many warriors like Angada and Jāmbavan were on his side. Hanumān was sent to explore the city of Laṅkā and bring back news of Sītā. He not only accomplished his task but also set fire to Rāvaṇa's huge capital and ravaged his groves. When Hanumān returned, after humbling Rāvaṇa, Rāma did not want to lose a moment, and at once set out with all his warriors, and with Vibhīṣaṇa, Rāvaṇa's brother, whom the demon-king had ill-treated, and who had joined Rāma's army. They reached the mighty ocean between the South coast of India and Laṅkā (Ceylon), and started building a bridge across the narrow straits for the army to go over. Here in the fourteenth part of Rāmacandrikā, the poet gives an imaginative description of the ocean, as Rāma and his army saw it.

41. Bhūti vibhūti piyushahu ko vish Īsha sharīra ki pāya biyo hai.
Hai kidhauṁ Keshav Kashyap ko ghar deva adevan ke man mohai.
Sant hiyo ki basaiṁ Hari santat shobh ananta kahāi kavi kohai.
Chandan nīr tarang tarangit nāgar kou kī sāgar sauhai.

The sea
is like god Mahādeva's body,[36]
containing
poisonous plants,
germs,
and the nectar-filled moon
reflected in its waters.

36. Śiva, Śaṅkara, or Maheśa—the Destroyer (see note 126). His body is smeared with ashes, and his neck blue from drinking the deadly poison which would have destroyed the world. (The sea is also blue, hence the analogy).

It is like the house of Kashyapa,[37]
and captivates the minds
of gods and demons
by its immensity.

The sea
is like the heart
of a saint
in which H ri[38]
dwel!s for ever :
no poet can describe
its eternal splendour.

The logs of sandalwood
bobbing on its billows[39]
seem like the wavy lines
of sandal-wood paste
upon the limbs
of men.[40]

42. Jal jāl kāl karālmāī timingalādik soṁ basai.
Ur lobh chhobh vimoh koh sakām jyoṁ khal ko lasai.
Bahu sampadā yut jāniye ati pātakī sam lekhiye.
Kou māṁgano aru pāhuno nahiṁ nīr pīvat dekhiye.

37. A Vedic sage to whom some hymns are attributed. He had a large part to play in creation, and is supposed to be the progenitor of mankind. The *Śatapatha Brāhmaṇa* says that he assumed the form of a tortoise and created offspring. He married Aditi and twelve other daughters of Dakṣa. As father of all creation he is sometimes called Prajāpati. He is one of the seven great *ṛṣis* and appears as the priest of Paraśurāma and Rāmacandra.

38. Hari is Viṣṇu, the Preserver (see note 162).

39. In ancient days traders used to cut logs of wood from the sandal-wood trees in Mount Malaya, float them in the waters of the narrow straits between India and Ceylon, and thereby take them to foreign lands. Hence many such logs kept floating in the sea.

40. Women of course anointed their bodies with sandal-wood paste in order to be perfumed, but men too used it. Vātsyayāna says : 'Now the householder, having got up in the morning and performed his necessary duties, should wash his teeth, apply a limited quantity of ointments

The huge carnivorous fishes[41]
living in the sea
are like evil thoughts
of lust, greed, anger,
delusion, and excitement,
in the mind
of a wicked man.

Though full of wealth
this ocean
is a great sinner,[42]
ostracised :
no mendicant
begs alms of it
no visitor drinks
its water.

Sunrise (From Chapter 5)

Sage Viśvāmitra came to Ajodhyā to meet King Daśaratha, with a purpose. He was conducting a Vedic ritual, but as soon as he would start, demons sent by the demon-king, Rāvaṇa, would come and upset it, so he wanted to take the king's son, Rāma, to kill the demons. Daśaratha reluctantly parted with him, and Rāma, along with Lakṣmaṇa, his brother, set out with Viśvāmitra for the forest.

and perfumes to his body, put some ornaments on his person, and collyrium on his eyelids and below his eyes, colour his lips with alaktaka (lac dye) and look at himself in the glass (Vātsyāyana, *Kāma Sūtra*, Tr. Sir Richard *Burton*, Luxor Press, London, p.14).

41. There are big carnivorous fishes in the sea which swallow smaller fishes. The smaller variety of fish are called *timi* (which the bigger ones swallow).

42. Great sins are of five kinds as enumerated by the Hindu Scriptures. These are killing a Brahmin (priest), consuming liquor, theft, committing incest with the wife of one's preceptor, and associating with one who has committed any of these sins.

After the demons had been slain by Rāma, Viśvāmitra wanted to take him to Mithilā, the kingdom of Janaka. Janaka was holding a svayaṁvara[43] *for choosing a suitable husband for his daughter, Sītā. She was to wed the prince who could string his bow. On the way they came across the retreat of sage Gautama, whose wife Ahalyā being afflicted by a curse had been turned into stone. Reviving her with his touch, Rāma crossed the river Gangā by boat, along with the sage and Lakṣmaṇa, and proceeded to Mithilā. As soon as they reached the boundary of the kingdom the sun arose. The description which follows is of the rising sun.*

Rāma :

9. Kachhu rājat sūraj arun khare.
Janu Lakshmaṇa ke anurāga bhare.
Chitvat citta kumudinī trase.
Chār chakor chitā sī lasai.

What Rāma said

The splendid red Sun
seems to be filled
with love
for Lakṣmaṇa
The Water-lily fears
he will touch her
with fiery
hands[44]

The *chakor*[45]
considers him
grievous
as a funeral pyre.

43. The choice of a husband by a princess made in public. Generally some feat of strength or skill was arranged, and the suitor who was successful wed the princess. In the present case the successful suitor had to lift and string the huge bow of King Janaka which bore a charm that only Rāmacandra could string it, and no one else.

44. The water-lily fears that the amorous sun may touch her with his hands. This is a fanciful concept of the Poet. Lilies open their petals with the rising of the sun, hence he is figured here as the lily's ravisher. (See also verse 11 in which this idea is further expanded).

45. The *cakora* is the Indian red-legged partridge who is believed to be enamoured of the moon and to eat fire. Of course the belief is purely fanciful and Hindi poets make frequent mention of the *cakora* in this context. There can be two interpretations of this line (a) The sun is

10. Arun gāt atipāt padminī-prāṇanāth bhaye.
Mānahu Keshavdāsa koknad kok premmaye.
Pari pūraṇa simdūr pūr kaidhaum mangal ghaṭ
Kidhaum shaktr ko chhatra maḍhyau māṇik mayūkh pāṭ.
Kai shroṇit kalit kapāl yah kil kāpalik kūl ko.
Yah lalit lāl kaidhaum lasat digbhāminī ke bhāl ko.

The crimson hued
early morning sun
has arisen.
It seems that the love
of the ruddy goose and the lotus[46]
which was within it
has spilled out.

Or as though
it is an auspicious jar[47]
painted all over
with vermilion.

Or Indra's umbrella
whose cloth
is woven
from the rays
of rubies.

Doubtless it is
a dreadful bloody head

like a funeral pyre and so provides a feast for the *cakora* who eats embers, (b) The sun is proving very troublesome for the *cakora* because he loves the moon, and it (the sun), has come out in the sky making the moon invisible, and is casting its burning rays in place of the cool moonbeams. Considering the context, the second interpretation is more suitable.

46. *Koka* means the *cakravāka* which is the Indian ruddy goose. Just as the *cakora* is believed by Hindi poets to be enamoured of the moon, so is the *cakravāka* bird said to be infatuated with the water-lily. In describing the love of women and men Hindi poets frequently use these examples.

47. Jars painted in beautiful patterns are kept in the pavilion in which a Hindu marriage ceremony is performed. Such jars are considered auspicious. Sometimes women stand with the jars on their heads singing songs. Auspicious jars also decorate pavilions in which public functions are held to welcome a distinguished guest or dignitary.

freshly severed for sacrifice
in a *kāpālik's* hands:[48]
    or a ruby
    on an eastern woman's
        forehead.

11. Pasare kar kumudinī kāj mano
Kidhaum̐ padminī ko sukh den ghano
Janu riksha sabai yahi trās bhage.
Jiya jāni chakor phaṁdāni ṭhage.

The spreading rays
of the Sun
seem like his hands
stretched out to clasp
the Water-lily
or to caress the young Lotus[49]
and give her joy.

The fear
of getting trapped
in the net
of the Sun's rays
has driven away
    the Stars:
        the Chakor too
        thinks the net
        to be a snare,
            and baffled,
                sleeps.[50]

48. *Kāpālikas* are *tāntric sādhus* who take liquor and eat flesh. They worship the goddess Kālī and offer in sacrifice often the heads of human beings. The rising sun is here compared to a human head covered with blood which has just been severed from the body and held in the hands of a *kāpālika* which he is soon to offer as sacrifice to the goddess.

49. The idea contained in verse 9 is continued in this one. The amorous Sun has now become more bold, and the rays, which are spreading from it as it rises, are imagined by the poet to be his hands which are stretching out to embrace his beloved, the water-lily, and to rouse the young small lotus and give her the intense pleasure of sexual union. *Kumudinī* means, a waterlily, and *padminī* or *kamalinī* means 'a small lotus'.

50. The *cakora* is said to be enamoured of the moon. So when he finds that the rays emanating are those of the sun an not of his beloved—the moon, he too like the stars, thinks it to be some kind of trap, and feeling cheated falls asleep.

Rāma:

12. Vyom meṁ muni dekhijai ati lāl shrīmukh sājahīṁ.
Sindhu meṁ baṛvāgni kī janu jvālmāl birājahīṁ.
Padmarāgani kī kidhauṁ divi dhūri pūrit sī bhaī.
Sūr-bājin kī kharī ati tikshatā tinakī haī.

What Rāma said

O sage,
see how splendid
the red sun is:
as though all the flames
of a submarine fire
were converging
to a point
in the sea.

Or as though
the sky was overspread
by the fine dust
of red rubies
ground by sharp hooves
of the Sun's horses.

Viśvāmitra:

13. Charho jagan taru dhāye, dinkar bānar arun mukh.
Kīnhoṁ jhaki jhaharāye, sakal tārakā kusum bin.

The red sun rising
skyward
causes the stars
to fade;
as a red-faced monkey
who, climbing a tree
and angrily shaking it,
makes its blossoms
fall.

Lakṣmaṇa:

14. Jahīṁ bāruṇī kī karī, vanchak ruchi dvijrāj.
Tahīṁ kiyo bhagvant bin, sampati shobhā sāj.

What Lakṣmaṇa said

(1) The moment
the Moon desires
to go west,
the Sun
robs him
of all his wealth
and splendour.

Or

(2) As soon
as a Brahmin
craves for wine,
God takes away
all his wealth
and splendour.[51]

Dawn (From Chapter 30)

After Rāma had slept the night in his palace lovely women sing softly at his doorstep to wake him up from his restful sleep. The things they say, and how the dawn comes, removing the darkness, is now narrated by the poet.

18. Jāgiye trilokdeva, devadeva Rāmadeva,
Bhor bhayo bhūmideva bhakta daras pāvaiṁ.
Brahmā man mantrabarṇa Bishnuhṛdaya-chātak phan,
Rudrahṛdaya-kamal-mitra, jagatgīta gāvaiṁ.
Gagan udit Ravi ananta, shukrādik jyotivant,
Chhan chhan chhabi chhīn hot, līn pīn tāre.
Mānahu pardesha desha, Brahmadosh ke pravesh,
Ṭhaur ṭhaur te vilāt jāt bhūp bhāre.

51. This verse has a double meaning, and both of them have been given in the text. *Vāruṇī* means, either (a) the western direction, or (b) wine; *dvijarāja* means, either (a) the sun, or (b) God. The former meaning viz. 'The sun robs the moon of all wealth and splendour as soon as he thinks of going west,' is more likely, as it fits in with the context.

O master of the three worlds,
Chakravartī,[52] King Rāma,
it is morning:
arise,
show yourself
to your devotees,
give charity
to Brahmins.

O Rāma,
Brahmā thinks of you
as eternal
and undecaying:
you please Viṣṇu,
and bring joy
to Mahādeva:
the whole universe
sings
your praises.

The sun has arisen
in the sky,
bright planets grow dim
each moment:
glimmering stars
disappear—
as mighty monarchs,
native
and of foreign lands,
slain
for the sin
of killing Brahmins.

19. Amal kamal taji amol, madhup lol ṭol ṭol,
Baiṭhat uri kari-kapol, dān-mānkāri.
Mānahu muni jñānavriddha, chhoṛi chhoṛi grah samriddha,
Sevat girigaṇa prasiddha, siddha-siddhi-dhārī.

52. A universal emperor, described by the *Viṣṇu Purāṇa* 'as one born with the mark of Viṣṇu's discus visible in his hand'. According to WILSON 'he who abides in or rules in an extensive territory, called a *cakra*'.

Taraṇi kiraṇi udit bhaī dīpjoti malin gaī
Sadaya hridaya bodh udaya jyoṁ kubuddhi nāsai.
Chakravāk nikaṭ gaī chakaī man mudit bhaī,
Jaise nij jyoti pāye, jīva jyoti bhāsai.

As soon as it is morning
swarms of restless black bees
fly away
from the lovely and delicate
lotuses:
and drawn by the ichor
of elephants,
alight on their foreheads.
they are like learned men,
ascetics, and saints,
who have renounced wealth and home
and live on famed mountains.

The lamplight
fades in the sun's brightness,
as understanding
in a compassionate heart
destroys depravity.

The *chakavi*
thrills with delight
to meet the *chakavā*,
as the soul shines
in the light of Brahmā.[53]

20. Aruṇa taraṇi ke vilās, ek doya uḍu akās,
Kali ke se sant Īsha, dishan ant rākhaiṁ.
Dīkhat ānandakand nishi binu duti hīn chand,
Jyom pravin yuvati hīn purusha dīn bhākaiṁ,
Nishicharchaya ke vilās, hās hot haiṁ nirās,
Sūr ke prakāsh trās nāsat tam bhāre.
Phūlat subh sakāl gāt, asubh sāil se vilāt,
Āvat jyoṁ sukhud Rāma, nāma mukh tihāre.

53. Brahmā or Brahman (as distinct from Brahmin=a priest) means the Absolute (see note 19).

Only one or two stars remain
when the red sun rises,
as in the *Kaliyuga*[54]
God keeps one or two pious saints
in each direction.

When night ends,
the moon,
deprived of its cheerful brightness,
is like a man helpless
without a clever wife.

The joys
of thieves and libertines
are destroyed,
as the murky darkness
slain
by the sun's light.

O Rāma,
as when your name is uttered
good things spread
and evil ones perish,
so auspicious works
prosper,
and wicked ones
disappear.

21. Sāro shuk shubh marāl, kekī kokil rasāl,
Bolat kal pārāvat, bhūri bhed guniye.
Manahu Madan paṇḍit rishi, shishya guṇan maṇḍit kari,
Apanī gudraini den, paṭhaye Prabhu suniye.

54. A *Yuga* is an age of the world. There are four *Yugas*—*Kṛtayuga*, *Tretāyuga*, *Dvāparayuga* and *Kaliyuga*. The *Kaliyuga* is the last one and it is, the *yuga* in which the world is now running. It commenced in 3102 B.C. and will endure for 432,000 years. It is believed to be an age of worry, distress, disease, decline of righteousness and religious worship, and general frustration.

Sodar sut mantri mitra, dishi dishi ke nrip vichitra
 Paṇḍit muni kavi prasiddha, siddha dvār ṭhāṛhe.
Rāmachanda-chanda or, manahu chitavat chakor.
 Kuvalaya jal jaladhi jor, chop chitta bārhe.

Starlings and parrots,
lovely swans and amorous cuckoos,
peacocks and sweet-voiced pigeons,
are singing in diverse notes:
it seems they are disciples
instructed by wise Kāmadeva,
and sent to you
 for being tested.

Therefore, O god, arise
and hear them.
Brothers, sons, friends,
ministers and kings of many lands,
scholars and renowned poets,
are standing at your door
desiring to have a glimpse of you;
as the lily, *chakor*[55], and sea-water,
 eager for the moon.

22. Nachat rachat ruchir ek, yāchak guṇa gaṇa anek,
 Chāraṇ māgadh agādh, birad bandi ṭere.
Mānahu manḍūk mor, chātak chaya karat shor,
 Taṛit basan sanyut ghan, Śhyām het tere,
Keshav suni bachan chāru, jage Dashrath kumāru,
 Rūpa pyāye jyāye līn, jan jal thal okai.
Boli haṁsi biloki bīr, dān mān harī pīr
 Pūre abhilāsh lākh bhāṁti loka lokai.

Beautiful dancers dance,
suppliants sing your praises,
bards, ministers, and captives,
eulogize your fame:

55. All the three, viz. *cakora*, lilies and sea-water, have a fascination for the moon. The *cakora* dotes on it, the water-lily opens when the moon is in the sky in the night, and tides are caused by the moon.

they are like frogs,
peacocks, and chakors,
who, taking you to be a dense cloud
charged with yellow lightning,[56]
speak to you
words of love.

Says Keśavadāsa,
when Dashrath's son
heard their charming voices,
he came out:
and all creatures of sea and land
revived when they saw him.

He talked and laughed with them,
giving charity to the poor,
respects to elders:
removing everyone's grief
in an instant,
and fulfilling millions of desires
of the people of the world
in one glance.

The Full Moon (From Chapter 30)

While Rāma and Sītā are admiring the beauty of spring from the palace, night comes. It is the full moon, and they admire its overpowering beauty. The description of the moon which follows is given by the poet through the words spoken by Rāma and Sītā.

Sītā :

41. Phūlan kī shubh gemd naī hai
Sūmghi Shachī janu ḍāri daī hai

56. A *pītāmbara* is a yellow silk cloth, or yellow silk clothes worn at the time of worship. Lightning is compared here to such a cloth.

Darpaṇa so shashi shrī Rati ko hai
    Āsan Kāma mahīpati ko hai.

What Sītā said

This moon
is like a ball of fresh flowers
which Indrarānī[57] had smelt
and cast away :
it is like Rati's looking glass
    or Kāma's seat.[58]

Sītā :

42. Moṁtin ko shrutibhūshaṇa jāno
    Bhūli gaī Ravi kī tiya māno.

Rāma :

Angad ko pitu so suniye jū
    Sohat tārahiṁ sang liye jū.

What Sītā said

This moon
is like a pendant of pearls
fallen accidentally
from the ear
    of Sun's wife.[59]

What Rāma said

No, he is like Bālī,
because he is always
    accompanied
by Tārā,[60] his wife.

57. Wife of Indra, the god of the firmament (see note 132).

58. Kāmadeva, the god of love (see note 158).

59. Sūrya the sun-god has three wives—Savarṇā, Svātī and Mahāvīryā. While sometimes Uṣas—the dawn, and Saṁjñā, daughter of Viśvakarmā are also mentioned as his wives. One of his several wives is here meant.

60. Tārā was the wife of the monkey-king Bālī and mother of Aṅgada. After the death of Bālī she married Sugrīva, his brother. There is a pun on the word, for *tārā* also means a star, and the stars are with the moon in the sky.

43. Bhūp manobhava chhatra dharyo jyoṁ
        Sok viyogini ko vidaryau jyoṁ
    Devanadī jal Rāma kahyau jū.
        Manahu phūli saroj rahyo jū.

What Sītā said

This moon
is like Kāma's umbrella
that's why the souls
of parted lovers
    are rent
when they see it.

What Rāma said

It seems to me like
a beautiful white lotus
    blossoming
in the heavenly Gaṅgā.

44. Phen kidhauṁ nabhsindhu lasai jū
        Devanadī jal hansa basai jū.
    Shankha kidhauṁ Hari ke kar sohai.
        Ambar sāraṁg te nikaso hai.

Is this the moon,
or a portion of the sky
reflected in the ocean ?
Or a swan
in the heavenly Gaṅgā ?
Or a conch
which has come out
from the celestial sea,
    and now finds splendour
    in Viṣṇu's hands.

45. Chāru chandrikā sindhu meṁ shītal svachha satej.
    Mano Shesha maya shobhijai hariṇādhishṭhit sej.

What Rāma said

This lovely moon
looks like Shesha's

cool and white lustrous bed
spread in the glittering
Kshīr-sāgar[61]
on which Viṣṇu himself rests.[62]

The Rains (From Chapter 13)

Travelling over many hills and through many valleys, Rāma and Lakṣmaṇa reached the Ṛṣyamūk Mountains. There they met Sugrīva, the ape king whose kingdom had been usurped by his brother Vālī. Rāma promised to slay Vālī for him and to recover his kingdom in return for Sugrīva's assistance in finding Sītā. The pact having been made, Rāma redeemed his promise, and slaying Vālī installed Sugrīva his friend, as king of the Kiṣkindha (Ape) country. Having done so, Rāma and Lakṣmaṇa decided to spend the rainy season in mount Malyavan about thirty-two miles from Sugrīva's capital. The description of the rainy season, and of autumn which follows, is given by Keśavadāsa in the words of Rāma and Lakṣmaṇa.

The rainy season in India follows the summer's unbearable heat, and starts with the outbreak of the monsoon in late June or early July. In the month of August (Sāvan) there is heavy rain. Dark clouds hover in the sky, and the peacock which delights in the coming of the rain, dances with joy. Sometimes, where the monsoon is heavy, it rains for days together and communication becomes difficult. Indians welcome the rainy season because it brings respite from the heat and from the hot looh wind. Describing the rain, Kālidāsa says in Ṛtusaṁhāra :

The silver clouds kiss the mountain-tops
and water rushes down valley and rill :
the peacocks move in the woods with joy,
and the green-clad hills look beautiful.

61. Sea of milk (see note 89).

62. The word *hariṇādhiṣṭhita* has a double meaning – (i) that on which Hari (Viṣṇu) is sitting, (ii) on which a deer (*mṛga*) is sitting. The black spot on the moon is supposed to be the shadow of a deer.

An anonymous Hindi poet describes the rainy season and its effect on lovers thus :

With pleasure filled the cuckoo sings,
the peacock cries with profound joy :
the lightning streaks from all sides,
and from dark clouds the rain pours :
The sparrow-hawk does not remain quiet,
and gales are speeding all round :
'tis Sāvan when with bosoms joined
the lovers' bliss is more blissful.

Similarly poet Bihāri describes thus the beginning of the rainy season :

Love awoke with the coming of the rain
and filled the hungry soul with sudden longing
to dally with women.
Dark clouds swiftly came low on the sun-baked earth,
as if to embrace that thirsty maiden,
and to kiss her face.

Here, however, the rainy season has been described in the context of Rāma's lamentation for Sītā. It reminds him all the more of her. So the unbridled joy which it usually brings is absent and the rainy months seem weary and hard to bear.

The coming of autumn brought new hope. The croaking of the frogs was still at last and thunder did not rumble any longer in the sky. The cheerful sun came out again. Rāma begins to get anxious, for Sugrīva has not come, and he is not able to set out on his quest for Sītā.

Rāma :

9. Chanda manda duti bāsar dekhau.
Bhūmahīn bhuvapāl visheshau.
Mitra dekhiye sobhat hai yoṁ
Rājsāj binu Sītahi hauṁ jyoṁ.

What Rāma said

The moon's light is dim
even on moonlit nights,

the day too is not bright;
both have lost their brilliance
as kings deprived
of their domains.

The Sun too shines
with subdued light:
he is much as I am
without my kingdom
and Sītā, my wife.

10. Patinī pati binu dīn ati, pati patinī binu mand
Chand binā jyoṁ jāminī, jyauṁ binu jāmini chand.

A woman is miserable
without her husband,
and a man dull
without his wife;
as the night
without the moon,
or the moon
without night.

11. Dekhi Rāma varshā ritu āī
Rom rom bahudhā dukhadāī.
Ās pās tam kī chhabi chhāī
Rāti dyaus kachhu jāni na jāī.

While Rāma was (in the forest)
the rainy season came
bringing him great grief
(because of separation from Sītā).
It is so dark
that day
can't be distinguished
from night.

12. Mand mand dhuni sāṁchan gājaiṁ.
Tūr tār jatu āvajh bājaiṁ.

Song of the Rains (By Nandalal Bose)

[to face p. 76

Ṭhaur ṭhaur chapalā chamkai yāṁ.
Indralok-tiya nāchati haiṁ jyāṁ.

The low rumble
of the clouds
is like the sound
of drums or cymbals:
the streaks of lightening
in many places
are like *apsarās*[63]
dancing
in Indra's heaven.

13. Sohaiṁ ghan syāmal ghor ghanai.
Mohaiṁ tinmeṁ bak pāṁti manai.
Sankhavali pī bahudhā jal syoṁ.
Mānoṁ tinako ugilai bal syoṁ.

The black and white clouds
are charming:
their swan-like fleeces
captivate the soul.

It seems while drinking
the sea's water
the clouds had swallowed
many conch-shells,
and are now disgorging them
with all their strength.

14. Shobhā ati shakra sharāsan meṁ.
Nānā duti dīsati hai ghan meṁ.

63. The *apsarās* are the celebrated nymphs of Indra's heaven. The name, which means 'moving in the waters' has some analogy to that of Aphrodite. They were produced when the ocean was churned for nectar. It is said that neither the gods nor the demons would have them, so they became common to all *surāṅganā* (wives of the gods) and *sumadātmajas* (daughters of pleasure). They are fairy-like beings, beautiful and voluptuous. They can change their forms at will, are fond of dice, and bestow freely their favours. Their amours on earth have been numerous. Famous *apsarās* are Urvaśī. Menakā and Rambhā.

Ratnāvali sī dividvār bhano.
  Varshāgam bāṁdhiya deva mano.

The rainbow is glorious,
the clouds are tinged
with many colours,
as though the gods have tied
a frill of gems
on heaven's gateway
  to welcome
  the rain.

15. Ghan ghor ghane dasahūṁ dis chhāye.
  Maghvā janu sūraj pai chaṛhi āye
Aparādh binā chhiti ke tan āye.
  Tinpīṛan pīṛit 'hvai uṭhi dhāye.

Dense clouds
have gathered all around,
as though Indra
had invaded the Sun,
for needlessly
  oppressing the earth.
  with summer's heat.

16. Ati ghātak bājat dundubhi māno.
  Nirghāt sabai pabipāt bakhāno.
Dhanu hai yah gauramdāin nāhiṁ.
  Sarjāl bahai jaldhār brithāhīṁ.

The cloud's thunder
is as the sound
of battle-drums :
the lightning crackles
as Indra's thunderbolt.

The rainbow
is like his bow:
the raindrops
  arrows

which he discharges
from it.

17. Bhaṭ chātak dādur mor na bole
Chapalā chamakai na phirai khaṁg khole.
Dutivantan ko vipadā bahu kīnhī
Dharnī kahṁ chandavadhū dhari dīnhī.

These are not toads
croaking,
or sparrow-hawks and peacocks
crying,
but Indra's warriors
challenging the Sụn to fight.

This is not lightning
which flashes,
but mighty monarchs
wandering about with drawn swords.
Filled with wrath
they have invaded the planets,
and capturing the ladybirds
made them over to the Earth
so that it can
avenge itself.

18. Taruṇī yah Atri rishīshvar kī sī.
Ur meṁ mand chandra prabhā sam nīsī.
Varshā na sunau kilkai kal Kālī
Sab jānat haiṁ mahimā ahimālī.

What Rāma said to Lakṣmaṇa

Obscured by clouds
the moon shines dimly
in the rainy season,
as Soma
in the womb of Atri's wife.[64]

64. Atri's wife is Anasūyā, and Soma (the moon) is said to be the son of Ṛṣi Atri by her. Soma is the Hindu god representing the *soma* juice (wine), an Indian Dionysus or Bacchus. In *Purāṇic* mythology he represents

The noise of toads
and crickets
is as the sweet laughter
of Kālī.

As Mahādeva is aware
of Kālī's great qualities,
so the serpents know
that the rainy season brings
many living creatures
for them to eat.

Varshā-Kālikā-rūpak

19. Bhauhaiṁ surchāp chāru pramudit payodhar,
Bhūkhan jarāye joti taṛit ralāī hai.
Dūri karī sukh mukh sukhamā sasī kī,
Nain amal kamaldal dalit nikāī hai.
Kesodāsa prabal karenukā gaman har,
Mukut suhansak sabad sukhdāī hai.
Ambar balit mati mohai Nīlkanṭh jū kī,
Kālikā ki varshā harashi hiye āī hai.

Comparison of the Rainy Season with Goddess Kālī

(1) In Favour of the Goddess

Is this the rain
or goddess Kālī ?[65]

The rainbows are
her lovely eyebrows,
dense clouds

the moon. *Soma's* chariot has three wheels, and it is drawn by ten horses of the whiteness of the jasmine, five on the right half of the yoke and five on the left.

65. The goddess Kālī or Devī (wife of Śiva) is represented 'with a black skin, a hideous and terrible countenance dripping with blood, encircled with snakes, hung around with skulls and human heads, and in all respects resembling a fury rather than a goddess'. (See note 128).

her big breasts,
lightning
the glint of her studded ornament.

Before the splendour of her face
the moon is dim:
her eyes
are brighter than lotus petals.

Her gait
is more graceful
than that of drunk elephants:
the jingle of her toe-ornament
is pleasing :
she wears a blue garment
        to charm
        Mahādeva.

(2) In Favour of the Rain

The rainy season
is delightful,
but brings
many dangers.[66]
The rainbow has come out,
dense clouds
        gather:
the swift lightning
lays bare
        earth and sky.

The moon has lost its lustre,
rivers turn muddy:
        lotus clusters
are torn apart:
        tanks
    are covered with moss.

66. The numerous dangers of the rainy season are the prevalence of snakes and scorpions which, due to the water entering their places of abode, come out in the open, the fear of houses falling due to heavy rains (in India quite a large number of houses are of mud, or so old that they can crumble down in a prolonged downpour), and last of all the danger from lightning.

The flow of rain-water, says Keshav,
has eroded pathways
and made them unusable :
the swans
have departed.

The sky
is overcast with clouds,
seeing which the peacocks
dance
with joy.

Is this the rainy season,
or the goddess
Kālī?

20. Abhisāriṇī sī samjhau parnārī.
Sat mārag meṭan kī adhikārī.
Mati lobh mahāmad moh chhāī hai.
Dvijraj sumitra pradoshmaī hai.

The big drains
which the rain-water forms
are like immoral *nāyikās*:[67]
as the path of virtue
is destroyed by them,
so does the current
wear down
good pathways.

67. A *parakīyā nāyikā* (*nāyikā*=a beautiful young woman) is one who cannot have her pleasure due to fear or consideration of society. An *abhisārikā* is a woman who, impelled by love, elation, and passion, goes to meet her beloved, or calls him to meet her. There are three kinds of *abhisārikās* (i) the *divābhisārika*, the woman who makes love by day, (ii) *śuklābhisārikā*, the woman who makes love in the moonlit night and (iii) *kṛṣṇābhisārikā*, she who makes love in the dark night.

As the *abhisārikā* woman leaves the path of virtue and shamelessly goes to meet her lover, so the rain destroys the good pathways (roads) by the force of its flowing water.

As a man
whose mind is obscured
by greed, pride, and passion,
harms Brahmins
and faithful friends:
so does the rain
hide the bright sun
and the moon
in a curtain
of darkness.

21. Barnat Keshav sakal kavi, visham gāṛh tam-sṛshṭi .
Kupurusha sevā jyoṁ bhaī, santat mithyā drishṭi.

Says Keśavadāsa,
the darkness is so dense
in the rainy season
that whether it is night or day
the eyes see nothing
as though by serving an evil man
one can have
no hope.

Rāma:

22. Kalhansa kalānidhi khanjan kanj kachhu din Keshav dekhi jiye.
Gati ānan lochan pāyan ke anurūpak se man māni kiye.
Yah kāla karāl te shodhi sabai haṭhi kai barshā mis dūr kiye
Abadhauṁ binu prāṇa priyā rahihaiṁ kahi kaun hitū avalaṁbi hiye.

What Rāma said

The moon
reminded me
of Sītā's face,
the mallard
of her gait,

the wagtail
of her lovely eyes,
and the lotus
of her feet :[68]
and kept me alive
for some days,
even though parted
from her.

But even these
were taken away
wilfully
by the rainy season:
now without the memory
of my beloved
how shall I
live?

68. Hindi and Sanskrit poets compare a beautiful woman's face to the moon, her gait to that of a mallard or swan, her eyes to the eyes of a wagtail, and feet to lotuses. Rāma therefore here compares the beauty of Sītā to these. The coming of the rainy season spoils the lotuses, for their tender petals are torn by the rain, and the moon is hidden by dark clouds. The swans and wagtails also are not seen. Therefore Rāma says that the rains have obstinately removed them.

The moon is a favourite comparison for the beauty of a woman's face. In the *Mahābhārata*, Urvaśī's face is described as being moonlike. In *Gita Govinda*, Jayadeva describes Rādhā's face thus: 'her face, a moon, is fondled like the fluttering petals in her hair'. Mālati is said to be moonfaced. Poet Bihārī says of a girl, 'Within her blue attire, her lovely face looks like the moon reflected in the rippling waters of a stream'.

The gait of Hindu woman is likened to that of an elephant or *rājahaṁsa* (a king goose or mallard). Queen Yaśomatī and Damayantī have a swan's gait, while Kālidāsa compares the gait of Indumatī to that of a swan. 'Your low sweet voice to nightingales was given your idly graceful movements to the swans'. In Jāyasī's *Padmāvat* when Padmāvatī went out to meet Ratansena, 'the swans departed when they saw her gait.'

The wagtail has big eyes, and so Hindi poets compare women's eyes to these. In Jāyasī's *Padmāvat* we have a description of the heroine coming to bathe with her companions in which her eyes are, 'like two wagtails sporting in the air'. Feet are compared to a lotus because of its softness and tenderness. Padmāvatī's rosy feet were like lotuses, and those of Rānī Vasumatī were like 'the lotus umbrella of the god of love'. In *Ṛtusaṁhāra* the anklets of the girls 'caressed their lotus feet'.

Autumn (From Chapter 13)

23. Bīte barshā kāl yoṁ, āī sarad sujāti.
Gaye aṁdhyāro hoti jyauṁ, chāru chāṁdnī rāti.

Autumn coming
after the rainy season
is as a lovely woman
of good family ;
and pleases the mind
as moonlit nights
after dark ones.

24-25. Dantāvali kund samān gano.
Chandrānan kuntal bhauṁr ghano.
Bhauṁheṁ dhanu khanjan nain mano.
Rājivani jyoṁ pad pānī bhano.
Hārāvali nīraj hīya ramaiṁ.
Janu līn payodhar ambar meṁ.
Pāṭīr juhnāihi ang dhare.
Hansī gati Keshav chitta hare.

Continuing the comparison of Autumn to A Lovely Woman (See Previous Verse), the Poet says

Her teeth
are as proud kunda flowers,[69]
her face
is as the moon :
her hair

69. The *kunda* flower is a kind of jasmine (*camelī* or Spanish jasmine), which blossoms during the hot and rainy seasons. It has middling sized white fragrant flowers and resembles more than any other species in leaf, flower, and fragrance, the common jasmine of the English gardens. Teeth are compared to it because of the flower's perfume, its pure white colour, and its glossy petals. The beautiful teeth of the girl who bore the betel-box of Mālatī gleamed like jasmine flowers. Kālidāsa describes girls who have teeth like jasmine.
'Dearest! God has certainly made both your eyes with lotus blue,
Your face too with lotus, teeth with jasmine, your lip with new twigs'.

is like a swarm of black bees,[70]
her eyebrows[71]
like bows of warriors
repaired,
and those new made:
her hands and feet
are like red lotuses:
the necklace
dangling on her bosom,
is of pearls
and *kumuda* flowers.[72]

She shyly hides her breasts
in her garment,
and anoints her limbs
with a paste
made of the moonlight itself.
She walks gracefully
with a swan's gait,
and captivates
the mind.

70. In India women generally have shining black hair which is comparable to black bees, and so Hindus frequently compare a woman's tresses to the black bee. Among the natural adornments of a young woman Bhartṛhari mentions, 'thick hair blacker than the black bee'. Kādambarī's hair was dark like a swarm of black bees, and a Sanskrit writer has the following fascinating description of a girl who has just got up from bed:

'The cascading hair of the doe-eyed
Just risen from the bed holding it
Tightly gathered in the cup of her hand
Seemed like a thick stream of black bees
Issuing out of a bowl.'

71. Eyebrows, which are arched, are compared to bows. Rādhā's eyebrows are compared to bows in *Gīta Govinda*. The brows of Padmāvatī when she grew of age, 'were bows from which she discharged coquettish glances'. Bhartṛhari describes sparkling-eyed women who shoot arrows of love from bows formed of their beautiful eyebrows. The brow of the woman seen by King Caṇḍa are described thus: 'her brow exactly resembled a bent bow, drawn to the very breaking point, as if to discharge a shaft'.

72. *Kumuda* is the white esculent water-lily which expands its petals during the night and closes them during the day. Hence it is known as the moon-lotus.

26. Shrī Nārada kī darasai mati sī.
Lopai tam tāp akīrati sī.
Mānau pati devan kī rati sī.
Sanmārag kī samajhau gati sī.

The autumn seems
like sage Nārada:[73]
as by his counsel
ignorance, misery,[74] and disrepute
are overcome,
so does autumn
end the darkness
heat and inaction[75]
of the rainy season.

27. Lakshmaṇa dāsī vriddha sī, āi sarad sujāti.
Manahu jagāvan ko hamahiṁ, bīte varshā rātī.

O Lakshmaṇa,
the autumn has come
like an old maid-servant
to remind me[76]
that the rainy season
has gone.

73. A *ṛṣi* to whom some of the hymns of the *Ṛgveda* are ascribed. In some respects he resembles Orpheus. He is the inventor of the *Vīṇā* (lute), and was the chief of the Gandharvas or heavenly musicians. He is known as 'strife-maker', and 'messenger, or spy'. He frequently arrives to advise gods and godly men when they are in trouble, and his counsel is very valuable though sometimes mischievous, and with a view to cause strife.

74. The word in the Hindi text is *tāpa* which means *trividha-tāpa* or *tri-tāpa*, i. e. triple misery—bodily ills, the sorrows which are given by God, and those caused by evil spirits.

75. The inaction is impediments caused to journeys, management of affairs of state, business, marches of armies for conquest, and so on. These are made difficult in the rainy season because of floods, waterlogging, and bad weather.

76. Old maid-servants were employed by princesses to w ake them up in the morning.

Spring (From Chapter 30)

This description of the spring occurs in Rāmacandrikā after Sītā has been rescued and Rāma has returned to Ajodhyā. After having their meals, Rāma and Sītā, rest on the balcony in front portion of the palace and enjoy the sights of spring.

32. Baiṭhe vishudha grah agraj agra jāya.
    Dekhi basant ritu sundar modadāya.
    Baure rasāl kul komal keli kāl.
    Māno ānanda-dhvaj rājat Shrī Vishāl.

Rāma went to rest
on the balcony of his palace,
and saw the beautiful sights
of spring.

The mango trees
in bloom,
are as though Kāma,
knowing it to be the time
for lovemaking,
had planted
    lovely perfumed,
        banners.

33. Phulī lavang lavalī latikā vilol.
    Bhūle jahāṁ bhramar vibhrama matta ḍol.
    Bol suhans shuk kokil kekirāj.
    Māno basant bhaṭ bolat yuddha kāj.

The blossoming
clove creepers and gooseberry bushes
sway in the breeze
restlessly:
drunk black bees
loll on them.

The swans and cuckoos,
parrots and peacocks

are like Spring's warriors
challenging everyone
to fight.

34. Sohai parāg chahuṁ bhāg uṛai sugandh
Jāte videsh virahījan hot andh.
Palāsmāl vinapatra virājamān.
Māno basant diya Kāmahiṁ agnibāṇ.

Men apply
fragrant powder
whose perfume
overpowers foreigners
parted from their beloveds:
the splendid clusters
of leafless *palāśa* trees[77]
are as though Spring
had made an *agnibāṇ*[78]
for Kāmadeva.

35. Phūle palās vilās thalī bahu Keshavdāsa prakāsh na thore.
Shesha ashesha mukhānal kī janu jvāl vishāl chalī divi ore.
Kiṁshuk Shrī shuktunḍan kī ruchi rāche rasātal meṁ chit chore.
Choṁchan chāṁpi chahūṁdis ḍolat chāru chakor agāran bhore.

The blossoms
of the *palāsa* trees
glisten
as though huge flames
emanate
from *Shesha's* mouths,
and go skyward.

77. The tree *Butea fondosa*, having beautiful purple flowers.

78. *Agnibāṇa* —a bow by shooting from which flowers of fire are produced which burn everything before them.

The *palāśa* flowers
red, like parrots' beaks,
are charming:
the *chakors*,
thinking them to be embers
take them in their beaks
and fly about.[79]

36. Khile ur sīt lase jaljāt
Jaraiṁ birahī jan jovat gāt.
Kidhauṁ man mīnan ko Raghunāth.
Pasāri diyo bahu Manmath hāth.

What Sītā said

O Rāma,
see how profusely
lotuses are flowering:
they are cool,
but the bodies of parted lovers
burn on seeing them.
It seems Kāma
has spread out hands
to grasp men's minds,
as a fisherman
catching fishes.[80]

79. The *cakora* is the Indian red-legged partridge which is said to be enamoured of the moon and to eat fire. The *palāśa* flowers which are flaming red are mistaken for embers by the *cakoras* and so they break them by their beaks and fly here and there with them.

80. For Kāmadeva see note 158. His banner displays the Makara. or a fish. The poet imagines that the lotuses are as if the god of love has stretched his hands to catch men's minds (which are likened to fishes) to decorate his banner with them.

Rāma's Beauty (From Chapter 6)

Rāma, and his bride Sītā, are sitting, surrounded by the women of the city. The occasion is their wedding. In the verses which follow Keśavadāsa describes the beauty of Rāma. This is an interesting section of Rāmacandrikā because Hindi poets, as indeed poets the world over, select women while describing beauty in the human form. This is one of the rare occasions when a man's beauty is described.

46. Gaṅgājal kī pāg sir, sohat shrī Raghunāth.
Shiva sir gaṅgājal kīdhauṁ, chandrachandrikā sāth

Rāma's white silk turban
seems as though
the Gaṅgā was encircling
Shiva's head:
    its water
    glimmering
    in the moonlight.

47. Kachhu bhrakuṭi kuṭil suvesh.
    Ati amal sumil sudesh.
Vidhi likhyo sodhi sutantra
    Janu jayājaye ke mantra.

Rāma's slanting
and symmetrical
eyebrows
are lovely,
  clear, and smooth:
they are like faultless
        mantras,
spontaneously written
by Brahmā
    to overcome others,
    and establish his
        supremacy.

48. Jadapi bhrakuṭi Raghunāth kī, kuṭil dekhiye jyoti,
Tadapi surāsur naran kī, nirakhi shuddha gati hoti.

Though Rāmā's eyebrows
are crooked,
gods and demons
on seeing them
attain *moksha.*

49. Shravaṇa makar-kuṇḍala lasat, mukh sukhama ekatra.
Shashi samīp sohat mano, shravaṇa makar nakshatra.

Rāma wears in his ears
splendid rings
shaped like fishes,
and it seems
the beauty of his face too
is concentrated there,
as though in the tenth zodiac
the moon
is shining
in its twenty-second mansion.[81]

50. Ati badan shobh sarasī surang.
Tahṁ kamala nain nāsā tarang.
Janu yuvati chitta vibhram vilās.
Tei bhramara bhaṁvat rasarūpa āsa.

The splendour
of Rāma's face
is like a limpid
lotus-pond.

His eyes
are lotuses,
his nose
the waves:

81. *Makra* is the tenth sign of the zodiac, and *Śravaṇa* the twenty-second lunar mansion. In this verse the poet has shown his knowledge of astrology. According to Hindu astrology, some portion of the lunar mansions of *Uttarāṣāḍha*, *Śravaṇa* and *Dhaniṣṭha* fall in the *Makara* zodiac, and this knowledge has been used by Keśavadāsa in his description of Rāma.

the minds
of young women
who enraptured,
gaze
on his beauty,
are like lovely black bees
hovering
to suck nectar :

51. Sobhijati dant ruchi subhram ur ānie
Satya janu rūp anurūpak bakhānie.
Oṭh ruchi rekh savisesha subh shrīrae.
Sōdhi janu Īsha subh lakshaṇa sobai dae.

His teeth sparkle
as though possessing
the radiance
of Truth,
His lustrous lips
are distinctive
and graceful
as though God
had given them
all good qualities.

52. Grīvā Shrī Raghunāth kī, lasati kambubar vesh.
Sādhu mano bach kāye kī, māno likhī trirekh.

Rāma's neck
is like a conch[82]
with three whorls
which are as lines

82. A beautiful neck is often likened by Hindi and Sanskrit writers to a conch with its three whorls. In Daṇḍin's *Daśakumāracarita* (Adventures of the Ten Princes), the neck of a girl seen by Prince Śaktikumāra was 'slender, and round as a conch-shell, wavy and lovely to look at'. The neck of Rānī Vasumatī is described thus: 'The conch-shell of the god of love went to the making of her flexible and slightly raised neck'.

Here the three whorls are likened to thought, speech, and action.

made by Brahmā
representing
thought,
speech, and
action.

53-54. Sobhan dīragh bāhu virājat.
Dev sihāt adevat lājat.
Bairin ko ahirāj bakhānahu,
Hai hitkārin ko dhanu mānahu,
Yoṁ ur meṁ bhrigulāt bakhānahuṁ.
Shrīkar ko sarsīruh mānahu.
Sohat hai ur meṁ maṇi yoṁ janu
Jānaki kī anurāgi rahyo manu.

His splendid long arms
make gods jealous,
and belittle demons;
they are like venomous serpents
for foes,
but for friends,
banners
of welcome.
The mark of Bhṛgu's foot-prints[83]
on his bosom
is like a lotus

83. Bhṛgu is a Vedic sage who is said to be the founder of the race of the Bhṛgus. It is related in the *Padma Purāṇa* that the *ṛṣis*, assembled at a sacrifice, disputed as to who was the deity best entitled to the homage of a Brahmin. Being unable to agree they sent Bhṛgu to test the character of various gods. He found Śiva engaged with his wife and so rejected him. Brahmā, to whom he next went, was surrounded by sages and was so much puffed up with vanity that he neglected Bhṛgu; so Brahmā too did not qualify. Lastly he went to Viṣṇu whom he found asleep. Indignant at the god's sloth he stamped upon his breast with his left foot and awoke him. Instead of being offended Viṣṇu gently pressed his foot and expressed himself honoured and happy by its contact. Bhṛgu was greatly pleased at the god's humility and proclaimed Viṣṇu as the only being to be worshipped by men or gods.

in Lakṣmī's hand :
the gem-studded medallion
dangling on his heart
is as though Sītā's mind
filled with his love
was reposing
there.

55. Sohat janarat Rāma ur, dekhat tinako bhāg.
Āye gayo ūpar mano, antar ko anurāga.

Those who see this medallion
are lucky :
Says Keshav, it seems
the love contained
in his heart
has spilled
out.

56. Subh motin kī dularī sudesh.
Janu Vedan ke āshar subesh.
Gajmotin kī mālā vishāl
Man mānahu santan ke rasāl.

The faultless pearls
of the two-stringed necklace
he wears,
are as the beautiful words
of the *Vedas* :

The large elephant-pearls
in his garland,
seem to be the minds of sages
full of tranquillity.

57. Shyām duū pag lāl lasat duti yoṁ tal kī.
Mānahu sevati joti Girā Jamunājal kī
Pāṭ jaṭī atī sant suhīran kī avalī.
Devanadī-kan mānahu sevat bhāṁti bhalī.

His black feet
and red soles
are as though
the Jamunā
and Sarasvatī
had met.

The row of diamonds
threaded with silk
on his shoes,
is as if
the Gaṅgā[84] too had come
to adore him.

58. Ko baraṇa Raghunāth chhabi, Keshav buddhi udār.
Jākī kirpā sobhijati, sobhā sab sansār.

Says Keśavadāsa,
who is so wise
as to be able
to narrate
the splendour of
Rāma
whose grace
glorifies
the whole world ?

84. The river Jamunā (sometimes spelt Yamunā) is deep, and so its water has a bluish hue. Hence the dark feet of Rāma are compared with its waters. The river Sarasvatī is also believed to be holy and was one of the boundaries of Brahmāvarta the home of the early Aryans. As a river goddess, Sarasvatī is lauded for the fertilising and purifying powers of her waters, and as the bestower of fertility, fitness, and wealth. (In later times Sarasvatī is the wife of Brahmā, see note 127). For Gaṅgā see note 3.

Sītā's Beauty (From Chapter 6)

Hindi poets are very fond of describing a woman's beauty, and there are certain standard similes which they use in doing so. For example eyes are compared to lotus flowers, eyebrows to bows, hair to black bees (because of their black colour), lips to the ripe red bimba fruit, breasts to gourds or the hard wood-apple, waist to a wasp, swan, or bamboo, gait to that of an elephant, neck to a conch, teeth to camphor or jasmine flowers, and forehead to the moon. In describing feminine beauty Keśavadāsa does not depart from the accepted norms.

After having described Rāma's beauty, the poet goes on to describe that of Sītā. His descriptions of Sītā are somewhat abstract and his comparisons rather far-fetched, but still they do not fail to depict the skill of his poetry.

59. Ko hai Damayantī Indumatī Ratī rātidin,
Hohi na chhabīlī chhanchhabi jo sigāriye.
Keshav lajāt jaljāt jātbed op,
Jatrūp bāpuro virūp so nihāriye.
Madan nirūpam nirūpan nirūpa bhayo,
Chand bahurūpa anurūpa kai bichāriye.
Sītā jī ke rūpa par devatā Kurūpa ko haiṁ.
Rūpa hī ke rūpak to bāri bāri ḍāriye.

Damayantī,[85] Indumatī,[86]
and Rati,

85. Wife of Nala and heroine of the tale of Nala and Damayantī. Nala was the king of Niṣadha and the story of Nala and Damayantī is one of the episodes of the *Mahābhārata*. The king won Damayantī, daughter of Bhīma, King of Vidarbha, at a *svayaṁvara* (choice of a husband by a princess in public) and lived happily for some time. Then one day at a game of dice he lost everything, even himself and his wife and children, to Puṣkara his young brother, and had to retire into the forest. After many adventures and hardships he was finally united again with his wife and won everything back in another game of dice in which he used the skill taught to him by King Ṛtuparṇa, an expert in the game. Damayantī was supposed to be very beautiful. The *Mahābhārata* describes her as, 'slender-waisted, shining amid her handmaids like the luminous lightning in the clouds'.

86. Sister of Bhoja, king of Vidarbha, who chose Aja for her husband at her *svayaṁvara*. She was killed by Nārada's garland falling upon her while asleep in an arbour. She was also famed for her beauty. (For Rati see note 13).

are no match
to Sītā,
even if clothed
night and day
with lightning.

The glint
of fire,
the lustre
of lotus flowers,
fades before her:
gold seems dull—
peerless Kāma,
being bodiless,[87]
can't compare;
and the moon
is a mockery.

Goddesses
seem ugly
when placed
beside her:
no comparisons
can do her beauty
justice.

60. Tahṁ sobhijai sakhi sundarī janu dāminī bapu maṇḍi kai.
Ghanshyām ko tanu sevahīṁ jaṛa megh oghan chhaṇḍi kai.
Yak ang charchit chāru chandan chandrikā taji chand ko.
Jan Rāhu ke bhaye sevahīṁ Raghunāth ānanda-kand ko.

87. The reference is to the reducing of Kāma, the Hindu god of love, to ashes by Śiva—the Destroyer. When Kāma obstructed the god's penance, Śiva reduced him to ashes by opening his third (middle) eye, and thus made him bodiless, after which he was called Anaṅga (*an*=without, *aṅga*=body). See also note 138.

At Her Toilet

[to face p. 99

Looking at
Sītā's lovely girl friends
one would think
the lightning
had left the clouds,
and taking
living forms
was attending on
Rāma.

One of the girls
has perfumed her body
with sandal-wood paste
and camphor:
her glamour is so great
that it seems
out of Rāhu's fear[88]
a moonbeam
has fled away
from the moon
to serve the blissful
Rāma.

61. Mukh ek hai nat lok-lochan lol lochan kai harai.
Jan Jānakī saṁg sobhijai shubh lāj dehahiṁ ko gharai.
Tahṁ ek phūlan ke vibhūshana ek motin ke kiye.
Jan chhīr sāgar devatā tam chhīr chhīṭan ko chhie.

One of Sītā's girl friends
demurely looks down,

88. Rāhu and Ketu are the ascending and descending nodes. Rāhu is the cause of eclipses. Mythologically he is a demon who is supposed to seize the sun and the moon and to swallow them, thus obscuring their rays and causing eclipses. The reason for his enmity is that when the gods produced nectar by churning the ocean, Rāhu disguised himself and drank some of it. The sun and the moon detected him and informed Viṣṇu who cut off his head and two of his arms. But as he had achieved immortality by drinking the nectar, his body was placed in the stellar sphere, the upper parts, represented by a dragon's tail, being Ketu the descending node. Rāhu wreaks his vengeance on the sun and the moon by occasionally swallowing them.

but keeps gazing
from the corners of her eyes,
drawing men's glances.

It seems Bashfulness herself,
taking a body,
is looking splendid
beside Sītā.

Other girls adorned
with flowers and pearls
are like goddesses
from *Kshīr sāgar*[89]
with splashes of milk
still on them.

62. Pahire basan surang, pāvakyut svāhā mano.
Sahaj sugandhit ang, mānahu devī Malaya kī.

One of the girls,
wearing a flaming
red dress,
seems like Agni
along with Svāhā.[90]

The body of another
is as fragrant
as that of a goddess
of Mount Malaya.[91]

89. One out of the seven seas which is believed to be a sea of milk, and the abode of Lord Viṣṇu.

90. Agni is the Fire-god of the Hindus and one of the chief deities of the *Vedas* to whom a great number of the hymns are addressed. His wife is Svāhā by whom he had three sons, Pāvaka, Pavamāna, and Śuci. Svāhā, which means 'offering', is the daughter of Dakṣa and Prasūti.

91. A mountain on which there are a number of sandal-wood trees, and which therefore bears a pleasant perfume.

Mandodarī's Naked Breasts (From Chapter 19)

After the death of Rāvaṇa's brother, Kuṃbhakarṇa, and Meghnād, his son, in the battle against Rāma's army, Rāvaṇa himself faced Lakṣmaṇa in combat. He discharged the bolt given by Brahmā against Lakṣmaṇa who fell into a swoon, but helped by Hanumān, was carried away from the field. Then the attack against Rāvaṇa was renewed, and his heart transfixed by a hundred arrows, he was borne away from the field by a charioteer of his army. After having recovered, Rāvaṇa began to make preparations for a sacrifice in order to achieve victory. Vibhīṣhaṇa informed Rāma about this, and Hanumān, Aṅgada, and other monkey warriors, were sent to disturb it. They boldly entered Rāvaṇa's palace and began to ransack it and to drag his wives, seizing them by the hair. Aṅgada did not know which of the women was Mandodarī, Rāvaṇa's chief wife. But when he caught one of the celestial nymphs who attended on her, she told him, out of fear. Then he caught Mandodarī by the hair and dragged her out of the picture-gallery. Her ornaments broke, the flowers in her braid were disarranged, and her brassieres torn, due to which her beautiful breasts spilled out. Here, poet Keśavadāsa gives a description of her disarray, and of her naked breasts.

80. Chhuṭī kaṇṭhamālā luraiṁ hār tūṭe.
Khasaiṁ phūl phailaiṁ lasaiṁ kesha chhūṭe.
Phaṭī kanchukī kinkinī charu chhūṭi.
Purī Kāma kī sī mano Rudra lūṭī.

Mandodarī's necklace
had fallen off,
her garland
had snapped,
the flowers in her braid
were scattered,
her hair was disarranged,
her brassieres torn,
and her gold waist-band
undone.
It was as though Shiva
had plundered
Kāma's city.

31. Binā kanchukī svachha bakshoj rājaiṁ.
Kidhauṁ saṁchahū shrīphalai sobh sajaiṁ.
Kidhauṁ svarṇa ke kumbha lāvaṇyapūre
Vashīkarṇa ke chūrṇa sampūrna pūre.

Are these Mandodarī's bare breasts
freed of brassieres,
or glorious
wood-apples ?

Or are they lovely pitchers of gold
filled to the brim
with the powder
of bewitchment ?[92]

32. Kidhauṁ ishṭadevai sadā ishṭa hī ke.
Kidhauṁ guchha dvai kāma sanjīvanī ke.
Kidhauṁ chitta chaugān ke mūl sohaiṁ.
Hiye hem ke hālgolā bimohaiṁ.

Perhaps they are the idols
of Rāvaṇa's family deities :
or bunches of flowers
of the *kāma* creeper :[93]
or two balls of gold

92. Hindi poets frequently compare the breasts of women to the *bela* fruit (wood-apple) which is a round fruit with a hard pale green rind varying in size from about that of a man's head to that of a tennis ball. Breasts are also compared to jars of gold. Bhūṣaṇa, a sixteenth century Telugu poet, describes the breasts of a girl, Girikā, thus:

'Her twin breasts, two pitchers of the purest gold
Spell beneficence for our whole planet'.

Vidyāpati, a famous Indian poet, would have an oath taken by a maiden's swelling breasts:

'I promise by the golden pitchers of your breasts
And by your necklace snake'.

Madanasenā's breasts are like 'pitchers half-revealed', and the breasts of one of Daṇḍin's heroines are described as shaming the ornate jars owned by King Anaṅga.

93. The ornamental climbing plant *Ipomaea Quamobit.*

resembling those
with which polo is played :
and as in that game
the eyes of the onlookers
follow the ball's course,
so do people look
wherever she turns her breasts.[94]

The Beauty of Rāma's Maid-servants (From Chapter 31)

In the morning Rāma sent for horses, and accompanied by Shuk, a friend, rode to his palace garden. They hid themselves in a secluded spot and watched the women sporting in the garden. Keśavadāsa describes the loveliness of the various limbs of Sītā's maid-servants and of the ornaments worn by them in the words of Shuk. Some of the verses describe the beauty of a particular girl, and others refer to all the maid-servants collectively.

(A) *Hair*

4. Rāma sang suk ek pravīno
Sīyadāsi guṇa barṇan vīno.
Kesha pās shubh syām sanehī
Dāsa hot prabhu ! jī videhī.

When they reached the garden,
Rāma's friend, Shuk,
praising the black hair
of Sītā's maid-servants, said,
it is so lovely and fragrant
that even ascetic's minds
would be enslaved by it.

94. The breasts of Mandodarī, Rāvaṇa's wife, are here compared to two balls of gold with which polo is played. Just as when the game is on, the players run to the place where the balls go, so do the minds of the onlookers move in the direction in which the beautiful woman's breasts are inclined.

(B) *Pigtail*

5. Bhāṁti bhāṁti kabrī shubh dekhī
 Rūpbhūsha-tarvāri visheshī
Pīya prem pran rākhan hārī
 Diha dushṭ chhal khaṇḍan kārī.

The pigtails
of the maid-servants
are as swords of handsome kings
to protect the love of husbands
and slay the cunning
 of villains.

6. Kidhauṁ siṁgār sarit sukhkāri.
 Banchaktāni bahā vanahāri.
Kanchan pānpāṁti sopān.
 Mano siṁgār lokā ke jān.

Are these pigtails,
or streams of adornment
which wash away
guile and cunning ?
the betel shaped ornaments
enlaced in them
seem to be stairs
leading to the world
 of beauty.

(C) *Ornaments of the Head*

7. Sīsphūl aru beṁdā lasai.
 Bhāg sohāg mano sir basai.
Pāṭin chamak chitta chauṁdhinī
 Mānau damakati ghan dāminī.

Her splendid head ornaments
are as though Fortune
and Married Bliss

had taken their abode
on her head.

The tangles
of her glossy hair
glisten,
dazzling the minds of onlookers :
as lightning
amid dark clouds.

8. Sundar māṁg bharī ati bhalī.
Tihi per motin kī āvalī.
Gaṅgā-girā tan soṁ tan jori.
Nikasīṁ janu Jamunā jal phori.

Her hair-parting
filled with vermilion,
and adorned with a string of pearls,
is splendid:
as though the currents
of the Gaṅgā
and the Sarasvatī[95]
had joined
burst through the black Jamunā waters.

9-11. Shīshaphūl shubh jaryo jarāya.
Māṁgaphūl sohai sam bhāya.
Veṇīphūlan kī bar māl.
Bhāl bhale beṁdā yuga lāl.
Tam nagarī par tej nidhān.
Baiṭhe mano bāraho bhān.
Bhrikuṭi kuṭil bahu bhāyan bharī.
Bhāl lāl duti dīsat kharī.
Mrigamad tilak rekh yugabānī.
Tinakī sobhā sobhit ghanī.

95. The black mats of hair are compared to the dark Jamunā's waters, the vermilion along the line of parting of the hair to the Sarasvatī and the string of pearls along the parting is likened to the River Gaṅgā whose water is bright.

Janu Jamunā khelat shubhgāth
Parsan pitahi pasāryo hāth.

What Shuk said

She wears twelve head ornaments—
a jewelled *shīshaphūl*,
and a *māṁgphūl*,
two *beṁdās* set with gems
and eight *benīphūls*—
which seem as twelve suns
in the city of darkness.[96]

Her coquettish eyebrows
which convey her varying moods
are prominent against her glowing forehead,
and the two lines of musk
between them
running up to her head ornaments,
are as the playful Jamunā goddess
stretching out her arms
towards her father,
the sun.[97]

(D) *Eyes*

12. Lochan manahu manobhava yantrahi.
Bhrū yug upar manohar mantrahi.
Sundar sukhad suanjan anjit.
Bāṇa Madan vishsoṁ janu ranjit.

96. In days past the fashion was to wear many ornaments. The ones mentioned in the stanza are all worn on the head or forehead. The *śīśaphūla* (*śīśa*=head *phūla*=flower) is an ornament for the head, the *māṁgaphūla* (*māṁg*=parting of the hair) is an ornament worn on the line from where women part their hair, the *beṁdā* is an ornament for the forehead, and *beṇīphūla* is another ornament for the head. Since the total number of ornaments worn by the woman are twelve, the Poet says that they seem like twelve suns shining in the city of darkness (the black hair).

97. The river Jamunā (or Yamunā) is said to be daughter of Sūrya (the sun).

Their eyes
are snares of passion,
their eyebrows
bewitching charms:
their lovely eyes,
painted with collyrium,
are like poison-tipped arrows
of Kāmadeva.

(E) *Nose*

13. Sukhad nāsikā jag mohiyo.
Muktāphalani yukta sohiyo.
Ānaṁdlatikā manahu saphūl.
Sūmghi tajat sasi sakalkushūl.

The girl's shapely nose
adorned with a pearl
charms all those
who see her.
It is like a blossoming creeper,
or as flowers
smelt and thrown away
by the Moon
to heal his pain.[98]

(F) *Ear-rings*

14. Tāṭank jaṭita maṇi shruti basant.
Rabi ekchakra rath meṁ lasant.
Janu bhāltilak-rabibratahiṁ līn.
Nriprūp akāshahiṁ dīpdīn.
Ati jhulmulīn sahjhalkalīn
Phaharāt patākā janu nabīn

The gem studded ear-rings
are as wheels

98. It is a popular belief that if a flower is smelt and thrown away it cures certain disease of the nose.

of Sūrya's chariot.[99]
It seems as though
a glorious king
moved by the fast undertaken
by the shining gems,
had given them the gift
of lighting heavenly lamps.[100]
The ear-rings and their pendants
glimmer
like new banners
waving.

(G) *Teeth and Mouth-odour*

15-16. Ati taruṇa aruna dvij duti lasanti.
Niju dāṛim bījan ko hasanti.
Sandhyāhi upāsat bhūmi deva
Janu bākadevi kī karat seva.
Shubh tinke sukh mukh ke vilās.
Bhayo upavan malyānil nivās.

Their firm and bright teeth
reddened with betel-juice,[101]
are like pomegranate seeds;
or as Brahmins
praying in the morning
to the goddess of speech.

When these girls
open their mouths to speak,

99. Sūrya is the Hindu Sun-god. He is represented as driving a chariot drawn by seven horses, or a horse with seven heads, surrounded by rays. His chariot is magnificent, having lovely wheels, hence here the gem-studded ear ornaments are compared to the wheels of his chariot.

100. The *ākāsadīpā* (sky-lamp) is a lamp fixed on a lofty pole which the Hindus hang for the gods in the *kārttika* (eighth) month.

101. *Pāna* means betels, which after being chewed, colour the teeth a brick red. In India many men and women chew betels constantly so that their teeth acquire a reddish hue.

the garden is filled with perfume,
rivalling
Mount Malaya.

(H) *Laughter and Speech*

17. Mridu musukāni latā man haraiṁ.
Bolat bol phūl se jharaiṁ.
Tinakī bāṇī sutimanahāri.
Bāṇī bīṇā dharyo utāri.

Their laughter
is charming
as a blossoming creeper,
when they speak
it seems as if flowers
are being shed
from trees:
their captivating voices
outvie the notes
of Sarasvatī's *vīṇā*.[102]

(I) *Curl of hair*

18-19. Laṭkai alik alak chīkanī.
Sūkshma amal chilaksoṁ sanī.
Nakmotī dīpakduti jāni.
Pātī rajinī hī unmāni.
Jyoti baṛhāvat dashā unāri.
Mānahu syāmal sīṁk pasāri.
Janu kabihit rabi rathe chhori.
Syāmapāṭ kī ḍārī ḍori.

There's a thin curl of hair,
smooth and bright,

102. Sarasvatī is the goddess of speech and learning, and patroness of the arts and sciences. She is frequently represented as playing on the *vīṇā*—an Indian stringed instrument, a kind of lute. Here the Poet imagines that the voice of the woman described by Śuka is so sweet that the goddess puts aside her *vīṇā* out of shame on hearing it.

on the forehead of one girl,
which seems as if Sūrya
has mistaken the pearl nose-pendant
for a lamp,
and the tangles of her hair
for night:
and pushed out a black stick
to praise the lamp's wick
and increase the light.[103]
Or as if he had dropped
a black silk rope
from his chariot
to pull Shukra[104] up.

Description of the Curl of Hair continued

20. Rūpa anūp ruchir rasabhīnī.
Pātur nainani ke putarīni.
Neh nachāvat hit Ratināth.
Markat lakuṭ liye janu hāth.

It is as though
with a sapphire stick in his hand,
Love, the tutor,
overpowered with the charm
of the pupils of the girl's eyes,
was teaching them to dance
so that they could see
love's god.

103. See note 96. In describing the ornaments of the head in the previous verses, Poet Keśavadāsa had mentioned the *śīśaphūla*, i.e., the head-ornament and compared it to the sun. Here, he says that the *śīśaphūla*-shaped Sun has mistaken the nose-pendant for a lamp and the hair on the head for night, and so to make light and dispel the darkness he has pushed out a black stick (the dangling black curl of hair), and having prised the wick of the lamp increased its light (i.e. the curl has increased the beauty of the pearl nose-pendant).

104. The planet Venus (see note 171).

(J) *Face*

21. Gagan chandra te ati baṛo tiya-mukh chandra bichāru.
Daī vichāri viranchi chit kalā chaugunī chāru.

Considering their faces
far superior to the moon,
Brāhmā has given them
four times more
grandeur.[105]

23. Ramaṇī mukhmaṇḍal nirakhi rākāramaṇa lajāya.
Jalad, jaladhi, Shiva, Sūr meṁ, rākhat badan chhipāya.

When the Moon
sees the faces
of these lovely women,
he feels so belittled
that he keeps hiding
in the clouds,
in the sea,
beneath Shiva's locks of hair,
and in the sun's orbit.[106]

(K) *The Ornaments of the Neck*

24. Bhūshaṇa grīvan ke bahu bhāṁtin sohat haiṁ.
Lāl sitāsit pīt prabhā man mohat haiṁ.
Sundar rāgan ke bahu bālak āni base.
Sīkhan ko bahu rāgini Keshavdāsa lase.

105. The moon is supposed to have sixteen digits while the face is here imagined by the Poet to have four times that number, i.e., sixty-four. Although all these sixty-four are not contained in the face, they are so many in number according to the *Kāmaśāstra* (art of love), and in learning or teaching them the mouth plays a part. Therefore the Poet has attributed them to the woman's mouth or face.

106. Whenever the moon is full it remains in the orbit of the sun. Hindi poets frequently compare a beautiful face to the moon. Here Keshava imagines the faces of Sītā's maid-servants to be so lovely that the moon is ashamed on seeing them and keeps hiding in various places.

The maid-servants wear
red, white, black, and yellow, ornaments
on their necks,
which charm men's minds
by their brilliance.

It is as though the sons
of the six Rāgās[107]
had come together
to learn different tunes.

(L) *The Arms*

25. Komal shabdanivant suvritta.
Alankāramaya mohanmitta.
Kāvya supaddhati shobhā gahe.
Inke bāhupāsh kavi kahe.

The graceful arms of these girls
are as the poetry
of a renowned poet.

The soft tinkling
of the ornaments
on their arms
are as the music of its words.

Their arms are round
and adorned,
like its beautiful
and ornate
stanzas.

Their husbands
are fascinated by their lovely arms,
as poetry lovers
are charmed
by such verse.

107. The *Rāgas* are the musical modes or melodies personified, six or more in number, and the *Rāginīs* are their consorts.

(M) *Hands*

26. Dekhahu deva dīn ke nāth.
Harat kusum ke hārat hāth.
Nav raṁg bahu ashoka ke patra
Tin maṁh rākhat rājkalatra.

What Śhuk said to Rāma

O lord, protector of the poor,
how strange it is that these maid-servants
can win over Sītā, their royal mistress,
by serving her
with hands so delicate
that they tire in plucking flowers :
whose fingers are tender
as new *aśoka* leaves.[108]

(N) *Ornaments of the Hands*

27. Sundar aṁgurin muṁdarī banī
Maṇimaya subaraṇa shobhā sanī.
Rājloka ke man ruchiraye
Māno kāmini kar kari laye.

On their lovely fingers
the girls wear
beautiful gold rings
inset with gems :
'tis as though
they had imprisoned
the minds
of the people of the royal household
in their hands.

108. *Sarca Indica* or *Jonesia*—an evergreen tree of considerable size with compact clusters of flowers varying in colour from pale orange to scarlet. The flowers emit a faint scent from far. Some varieties do not flower but have soft tender leaves.

(O) *Breasts*

28-29. Ati sundar ur pai urjāt.
Shobha sarmeṁ janu jaljāt.
Akhil loka jalmaya karidhare.
Bashī karaṇa chūraṇa chaye bhare.
Kāma Kuṁwar abhishek nimitta.
Kalasha rache janu yauvan mitta.
Kāma-keli-kanduk kamanīya.
Mano chhipāye Rati nij hiya.

Their beautiful jutting breasts
are like lotuses
flowering in the sea
of splendour.
Thinking them to be filled
with the powder of bewitchment,
men are disheartened.[109]

They are like gold jars
made for sprinkling
scented water
on the Prince of Love:
or two balls
for Kāma to play with,
which Rati had hidden
in her bosom.

30. Romarāji siṁgāri kī lalit latā kī rāj.
Tāhi phale kuchrūp phal lai jagjyoti samāj.

The line of hair
above the navel
is as a lovely creeper
of adornment,
on which the breasts

109. The onlookers are sad because the breasts of the maid-servants are very bewitching but beyond reach. and they cannot be enjoyed.

are like two fruits
containing
all the world's
splendour.

(P) *Line of Hair extending across the Navel*

31. Sūkshma romovalī subesh.
Upamā dīnhī Shuk savishesh.
Ur meṁ manahu Madan kī rekh
Tākī dīpati dipati ashesha.

The thin row of hair
above their navels
shine,
as though they were lines of passion
in their hearts.

(Q) *Waist*

32. Kaṭi ko tattva na jāniye suni prabhu Tribhuvan rāva.
Jaise suniyat jagan ke sat aru asat subhāva.

What Shuk said

Listen, Rāma,
as in this world
we hear about truth and untruth,
but do not quite understand
the difference;
so it is heard
that these girls have waists,
but on seeing
they appear not to have them.

(R) *Buttock, Waist and Thigh*

33. Nitamb bimba phūl se kaṭipradesh chhīn hai.
Bibhūti lūṭi lī sabai sulok lāj līn hai.

Amoḷ ūjare udār jangh yugma jāniye.
Manōj ke pramod soṁ vinod yantra māniye.

Their hips
are swollen with joy:
it seems they have robbed
the poor waists,
who have become lean
with sorrow,
and hide
from men's gaze.

Their thighs,
sturdy, firm,
fair, and matchless:
are like two toys
for Kāma to play with
at the time of lovemaking.

(S) *Feet*

34. Chhavān kī chhuī na jāti shubhra sādhu mādhurī.
Biloki bhūli, bhūli jāt chitta chāl āturī.
Vishuddha pāda-padma chāru angulī nakhāvali
Alakta yukta mittra kī suchitta baiṭhakī bhalī.

Their heels are so fair and spotless
that I fear they will be sullied
even by the touch
of the eye's gaze[110];
the mind forgets
its restless nature
and stays with them.

(T) *Red Lac-dye*

35. Kaṭhin bhūmi ati koṁvare jāvak yut shubh paye.
Janu pahirī, tantrāṇa ko, māṇik tarī banāya.

110. The heels cannot be touched by the eyes because it is feared that by the contact of sight they will become dirty. A fanciful conception of the Poet.

The red dye
on their tender feet
seems like shoes of rubies
which they have worn
to protect them
from the hard ground.

(U) *Brassieres*

36. Varaṇa varṇa aṁgiyā ur dhare.
Madan manohar ke man hare.
Anchal ati chanchal ruchi rachaiṁ.
Lochan chal jinke saṁg nachaim.

They are wearing
brassieres of different colours
which charm even Kāma's mind.
Looking at their lovely end-cloths
flying in the wind
beholders feel
giddy.

(V) *Ornaments of the Entire Body*

37. Nakh shikh bhūshit bhūshanani, paṛhi subaraṇamaya mantra.
Yauvanshrī chal jāni janu, bāṁdhe rakshā-yantra.

The gold ornaments
with which their limbs are loaded,
seem talismans
charged with *mantras*,
which they have worn
to bind youth eternally,
fearing it will escape.

(W) *Beauty af the Entire Body*

38. Mohan shaktin aisī
Mīndhujā-dhuj jaisī.

Mantra bashīkar sājaiṁ
Mohanmūri birājaiṁ.

What Śhuk said to Rāma

Should I compare them
to goddesses of charm ?
or to banners of love's god ?
or to articles for an oblation
performed to obtain
the *mantras* of bewitchment ?
or are they herbs
of enchantment?
To what should I compare
these lovely girls ?

(X) *Power of Beauty*

39. Bhāl meṁ bhav rākhiyo shashi kī kalā shubh ek.
Toshata upajāvatīṁ mriduhās chandra anek.
Mār ek viloki kai har jāri kai kiya chhār.
Nainkor chitai karaiṁ patichitta mār apār.

Shiva bears only one moon
on his forehead,
while the laughter
of each maid-servant
gives the delight
of many moons.

Shiva reduced love's god
to ashes
by a glance of his third eye,
but by one sidelong glance
these girls create
countless desires
in their husbands' minds.

(Y) *Splendour of the Limbs*

40. Kanṭak aṭkat phaṭi phaṭi jāt.
Uṛi uṛi basan jāt basha bāt.

Taū na tinke tan lakhi pare.
Maṇigaṇa ang ang prati dhare.

The thorns tear their dresses,
the wind blows them away;
yet their uncovered limbs
can't be seen
because the numerous gems
set in their ornaments
dazzle the eyes.

(Z) *Incomparableness*

41. Upamāgan upajāya Hari, bagarāye sansāra.
Inko parasparopamā, rachi rākhīṁ kartār.

What Shuk said to Rāma

O Rāma, Brahmā has created
many metaphors for women,
and spread them all over the world;
but not one of them
is good enough for these maid-servants—
their beauty can be compared only
with each others'.

The Water Sport (From Chapter 32)

The scene of the water sport is the pond near Rāma's palace. Rāma, Sītā, and Sītā's maid-servants, take part in it, and entering the pond engage in all sorts of frolics, which have been charmingly described by Keśavadāsa.

37. Ek Damayantī aisī haraiṁ haṁsi haṁs vansha,
Ek hansinī sī bisahār hiye rohiyo.
Bhūshaṇa girat ekai letī būṛi bīchi bīch
Mīn gati līn hīn upamān sohiyo.

Ekai mat kaikai kanṭh lāgi lāgi būṛi jāt,
Jal devatā sī devi devatā vimohiyo.
Keshodāsa ās pās bhaṁvar bhaṁvat jal-
Keli meṁ jaljamukhī jaljasī sohiyo.

A girl laughs,
and like Damayantī,
catches hold of swans:
another picks up a lotus root,
as a female swan would,
wraps it playfully
round her neck.

Yet another girl dives,
and moving more swiftly than a fish
retrieves her ornament
while it is yet in the water.

Some girls plunge down
arm in arm
to see who can remain longest
under water.

They are like sea goddesses,
and charm
even the heavenly nymphs.
Says Keshavdāsa,
while sporting in the pond
these moonfaced girls
look like lotuses,
and deceived, the black bees
keep hovering
around them.

38. Krīṛā sarvar meṁ nripati, kīnhī bahu bidhi keli.
Nikase taruṇi samet janu, sūraj kiraṇa sakeli.

Rāma sported in the pond
in many ways,
and when he was satiated
he came out

along with all the girls,
looking like the sun god
with all his rays
gathered.

Women After Bathing (From Chapter 32)

After having sported in the pond the girls came out. The water sport had loosened some of their ornaments, which had fallen into the pond, and had also spoilt their make-up.

39. Nīradhi te nikasīṁ tiya jabai.
Sohati haiṁ bin bhūshaṇa tabai.
Chandan chitra kapolan nahīṁ.
Pankaj Keshav sohat tahīṁ.

When the girls came out
they found that some of their ornaments
had fallen into the pond:
yet they looked
very lovely.

The patterns of sandal-wood paste
which adorned their cheeks
had been washed off,
and lotus filaments
had got stuck to them.

40. Motin kī bithurī shubh chhaṭaiṁ.
Haiṁ urjhī urjātan laṭaiṁ.
Hās siṁgār latā manu bane
Bheṁṭat kalpalatā hit ghane.

The strings of pearls
loosened from their braids,
along with the locks
of their disordered tresses,

had got entangled
with their breasts.
It was as though
laughter and love
becoming creepers,
had met the wishing creeper[111]
lovingly.

41. Keshani orani sīkar ramaiṁ.
Rikshani ko tamayī janu bamaiṁ.
Sajjal aṃbar chhoṛat bane.
Chhūṭat haiṁ jal ke kaṇa ghane.
Bhog bhale tan soṁ mili kare.
Chhoṛat jāni te rovat khare.

Drops of water fall
from the ends of their hair,
as though Night
were disgorging planets.

Their wet garments
can now uncleave.
The water dripping
from their clothes
is as though recollecting
their great pleasure
when joined to the lovely limbs of the girls,
they were weeping
to part from them.

111. *Kalpalatā* (*Kalpavṛkṣa* or *Kalpataru*) is the wishing tree or creeper, a mythical tree in heaven, which is believed to grant all desires.

Lady With Mirror (Indian Sculpture)

[to face p. 122

The City of Ajodhyā (From Chapter 1)

The description of Ajodhyā city[112] *occurs in the first chapter of the book. After having observed the beauty of King Daśaratha's garden, Viśvāmitra, accompanied by many other sages, 'whose visage shone as the glow of a fire,' goes to see the grandeur of the city of Ajodhyā—the capital of Daśaratha's kingdom.*

37. Uṁche abās
Bahu dhvaj prakās.
Sobhā bilās.
Sobhai prakās.

Diverse flags
wave
on the tall houses,

112. Ajodhyā is one of the holy cities of India and a place of pilgrimage. In *Rāmāyaṇa* Tulasīdāsa says about it, 'In all the universe this city is renowned, and very holy. In the world there are four kinds of creatures—those born from eggs, those born from sweat, those born from sprouts, and those born from the womb. Of these whoever dies in Ajodhyā is never again born in the world and achieves emancipation' (Tulasīdasa, *Rāmāyaṇa*, *Bālakāṇḍa*, 34.2).

The Fyzabad Gazetteer has the following account: 'That a kingdom of Kosala, with its capital at Ajodhya, existed sometime before the birth of Christ, is, however, certain. Ajodhya was also an important city in Jain literature—the first, second, fourth, fifth and fourteenth Tirthankaras are said to have been there... Ajodhya is undoubtedly a place of immense antiquity... The city is intimately connected with the mass of legend referring to Rāmchandra of the Solar race, and was certainly the capital of several reigning dynasties... The sacred places of Ajodhya are exceedingly numerous. The spot, according to Hindu mythology, represents the forehead of Viṣṇu and is the seat of learning and the chief of the seven *tīrthas*. It is undoubtedly the most important centre of Viṣṇu worship in Oudh, if not in the whole of Upper India, and claims precedence over Mathura and Hardwar. It is only natural, therefore, that the sacred places connected with Viṣṇu in his various incarnations, and especially that of Rāmacandra the best known of all, should be many in number and should spread beyond the immediate precincts of the city...' (*Fyzabad : A Gazetteer* H. R. NEVILL, Allahabad, 1905).

countless decorations
reveal
the city's
splendour.

38. Ati sundar ati sādhu.
Thir na rahat pal ādhu.
Param tapomaye māni.
Daṇḍadhāriṇī jāni.

Very beautiful,
absolutely straight,
and continually
waving,
the flags
are like
ascetics :
for as ascetics
doing penance,
hold a rod,
and stand on one leg ;
so these flags
wave
on single
flagstaffs.

39. Shubh Droṇa giri maṇi shikhar
Upar udit aushadhi so ganau.
Bahu vāyu vash vārid bahorahi
Arujh dāmini duti manau.
Ati kidhauṁ ruchir pratāp
Pāvak pragaṭ surpur ko chalo.
Yah kidhauṁ sarit sudesh merī
Karī divi khelat bhalo.

What Viśvāmitra said

The red flags
are like the gleam
of celestial herbs

of Mount Droṇāchal :[113]
or as though the wind
was sending back
to the clouds,
lightning
which had got entangled
in the flagstaffs:
or as the light
of the great race
of Raghus[114]
rising heavenward.

The white flags are
as though the River Kaushiki,[115]
which I created,[116]
was sporting
in the sky.

Describing the White Banners, Visvāmitra says

40. Jīti jīti kīrati laī, shatrun kī ḅahu bhāṁti.
Pur par bāṁdhī shobhijai, mānyu tinkī pāṁti.

113. A mountain,(also called Droṇagiri mentioned in the *Rāmāyaṇa*) on which Hanumān, the monkey god, went to fetch the herb, *sañjīvanabūṭī* to cure Rāma's brother, Lakṣmaṇa, when the latter was grievously wounded by Rāvaṇa's spear. In this verse the extreme height of the houses of the city has been depicted.

114. Raghu is the name given to a king of the Solar race. According to the *Raghuvaṁśa* he was son of Dilīpa and great-grand father of Rāma. who from Raghu got the patronymic Rāghava and the title Raghupati, chief of the race of Raghu.

115. A river in Bihar, also called the Chandika or Kosi. Satyavatī, daughter of King Gādhi, wife of the Brahmin Ṛcīka, mother of Jamadagni, and grandmother of the sage Paraśurāma, who was of the Kuśika race, is said to have been transformed into the Kauśikī river.

116. 'I' here means the sage Viśvāmitra. It is he who is describing the city of Ajōdhyā. One account considers him to be son of King Kuśika, a descendant of Kuśa (see note 1). As Satyavatī, who too was of the Kauśika race (see previous note 115), is said to have been transformed into the River Kauśikī. the sage claims to be its creator.

It seems King Dashrath,
having vanquished his foes,
has snatched their reputes,
and planted them in rows
as white
banners.

41. Sam sab ghar shobhaiṁ muni man lobhaiṁ ripugaṇa chhobhaiṁ dekhi sabai.
Bahu dundubhi bājai jan ghan gājaiṁ diggaj lājaiṁ sunat jabai.
Tahṁ tahṁ shruti paṛhahīṁ vighan na baṛhahīṁ jaye yash maṛhahīṁ sakal dishā.
Sabaī sab vidhi ' ksham basat yathākram devapurī sam divas nishā.

All houses are of the same height,
their evenness
gladdens sages,[117]
and grieves foes.

The sound of kettledrums
resounds all over
as the thunder
of clouds,
shaming the elephants
of the eight quarters.[118]

At many places
priests chant the *Vedas*,[119]

117. Sages are free from the emotions of desire and aversion, and hence they like evenness of mind. Therefore it is said here that the uniformity and equal height of the houses appeals to sages.

118. The mythical elephants who are believed to support the earth (see note 150).

119. *Veda* is from the Sanskrit root *vid*-'know'. The *Vedas* are holy books which are the foundation of Hindu religion. They were composed between 1500 and 1000 B. C. or even earlier, and are believed to be of divine origin, and revealed to the *ṛṣis* or sages. There are four *Vedas*, *Ṛg* *Yajur*, *Sāma*, and *Atharva,* the one of most ancient origin being the *Ṛgveda*.

dispelling
ills.

The worthy citizens,
fortunate and courageous,
live methodically:
so that this city
rivals
Devapurī.[120]

42. Kavikulvidyādhar, sakal kalādhar, rājrāj var besh bane.
Gaṇapati sukhdāyak, pashupati lāyak, sūr sahāyak kaun ganai.
Senāpati budhjan, mangalgurugaṇa, dharmarāl manubuddhi dhanī.
Bahu shubh mansākar, karuṇāmaya aru sūrat-ranginī shobhsanī.

In this city live
scholars and poets,
men knowing all the fine arts,
skilled sculptors,
handsome Kshatriyas,[121]
courteous officers,
worthy grooms, mahouts,

Each *Veda* is divided into two parts—*Mantra* and *Brāhmaṇa*, the former consisting of hymns embodying prayer and praise, and the latter containing liturgical and ritualistic glosses, explanations, and applications of the hymns illustrated by numerous legends. To the *Brāhmaṇas* are added the *Āraṇyakas* and *Upaniṣads*, philosophical and mystical treatises in prose and verse, which are the bedrock of Hindu philosophy.

120. The capital of Indra's heaven, renowned for its greatness and splendour. (Indra is the Hindu god of the firmament.) It is situated somewhere in the vicinity of Meru (a fabulous mountain in the navel or centre of the earth-the Olympus of the Hindus). The city is also known as Devapura, 'city of the gods', and Pūṣabhāsā 'sun-splendour'.

121. Hindu society is divided into four castes or *varṇas* by Manu. There are Brahmins—the priestly and learned caste—who consider themselves 'twice-born' and the highest; Kṣatriyas—the regal and warrior class; Vaiśyas—the traders and agriculturists; and Śūdras, the servile caste whose duty is to serve the others.

and the like,
brave warriors
and countless others
engaged
in service.

Excellent commanders of armies,
pundits
and Brahmins who recite the Scriptures,
learned judges,
and charitable men
who give alms to the poor,
live in this city;
and nearby
the charming Saryū[122]
flows.

43. Paṇḍit gaṇa maṇḍit gaṇa daṇḍit mati dekhiye.
Kshatriyavar dharma pravar kruddha samar lekhiye.
Vaishya sahit satya rahit pāp pragaṭ māniye.
Shūdra sakati vipra bhagati jīva jagat jāniye.

The Brahmins
living in the city
have goodness and learning:
The Kshatriyas
are staunch in their duties,
and show anger
only in battle:
The Vaishyas
are truthful and upright:
and there is awakening
in the minds of
Shūdras.

44. Ati muni tan man tahm̐ mohi rahyau.
Kachu budhi bal vachan na jāye kahyau.
Pashu pakshi nāri nirakhi tabai
Din Rāmacandra guṇa ganat sabai.

122. The same as the River Sarajū (see note 2).

Viśvāmitra was charmed
by the wonderful city,
he had not words enough
to praise it.

Further he saw
that the men and women,
birds and beasts,
and all living creatures in it,
extolled Rāma's goodness
all day.

45. Ati uchcha agārani banī pagārani janu chintāmaṇi nāri.
Bahu shat makh-dhūmani-dhūpit angaṇ Hari kī sī anuhāri.
Chitrī bahu chitrani param vichitran Keśavdāsa nihāri.
Janu viśvarūpa ko amal ārasī rachī biranchi bichāri.

The precious stones inlaid
in the boundary walls
around the towering houses
seem like collections
of fabulous gems.[123]

The smoke
of hundreds of oblations
have perfumed the courtyards
and made them black
like Viṣṇu's complexion.

The walls of many houses
are covered with curious paintings.

123. *Cintāmaṇi* is the 'wish-gem'. It is a jewel which is believed to have the power of granting all desires—the philosopher's stone. It is said to have belonged to Brahmā, who himself is called by this name (*Cintāmaṇi*). It is also called *divya-ratna*. The large number of dazzling gems with which the walls of the houses were studded appeared like so many *Cintāmaṇis*.

Says Keshav, the houses seem
as if Brahmā[124] had made a stainless mirror
for viewing the world.

46. Jag yashvant vishāl, rājā Dashrath kī purī.
Chandra sahit sab kāl, bhālthalī janu Īsh kī.

King Dashratha's city
is renowned
throughout the world
for Rāma[125] lives there.
It is like Mahādeva's[126] forehead
containing the moon.

124. The first member of the Hindu triad—the Creator of the universe. When Brahmā has created the world it remains unaltered for one of his days, which is a period of 2,160,000,000 years. Thereafter it is consumed by fire—the sages, gods, and the elements surviving—and afterwards again restored. This process goes on till his existence of a hundred years. After this he himself expires, and all the gods, and sages: and the whole universe is resolved into their constituent elements.

Brahmā is said to be of red colour, having four heads and four arms. His consort is Sarasvatī, goddess of learning, (also called Brāhmī), his vehicle is a swan or goose, and he lives in Brahma-vṛndā. Unlike other gods he is not widely worshipped, though his name is invoked in religious services.

125. Son of Daśaratha, and the hero of the *Rāmāyaṇa* (see note 1).

126. The 'great-god'. A name for Śiva (Maheśa or Śaṅkara), one of the Hindu triad—the Destroyer. He is the 'lord of songs, the lord of sacrifices, who heals maladies, as brilliant as the sun, the best and most bountiful of all gods, who grants prosperity and welfare to horse and sheep, men, women, and cows; the lord of nourishment, who drives away diseases, dispenses remedies, and removes sin: but on the other hand he is the wielder of the thunderbolt, the bearer of bows and arrows, and mounted on his chariot, is terrible as a wild beast, destructive and fierce'. He is a fair man with five faces and four arms. He is commonly shown seated in profound thought with a third eye in the middle of his forehead, contained in, or surmounted by, the moon's crescent. His matted locks are gathered up into a coil like a horn, which bears upon it a symbol of the river Gaṅgā, which he caught as it fell from heaven. He has many names and temples dedicated to him, and is also represented as a phallus.

Here the meaning is, that because Rāmacandra lives in Ajodhyā, the city appears as the unblemished moon on the second day of the lunar fortnight, adorning the forehead of Śiva.

47. Paṇḍit ati sigarī puri mānahu girāgati gūṛh.
Singha caṛhī janu chaṇḍikā mohati mūṛh amūṛh.
Mohati mūṛh amūṛh devasang 'diti jyauṁ sohai.
Sab śṛṅgār sadesh mano Rati Manmath mohai.
Mano Śachī Vidhi rachī vividh vidhi varṇat paṇḍit.

The wisdom
of its citizens
is like Sarasvatī[127]
in hiding,
or as Durga[128]
seated on a lion,
seeing whom foolish men are terrified
and wise men charmed.[129]

The city
and its people
are attractive
as Aditi[130]
with all the gods.

127. The wife of Brahmā, the goddess of speech and learning, inventress of the Sanskrit language and Devanāgarī letters, and patroness of the arts and sciences. 'She is represented as of a white colour, without any superfluity of limbs, and not infrequently of a graceful figure, wearing a slender crescent on her brow and sitting on a lotus'. (*Wilson*)

The meaning contained in the line is that the people of the city are very wise but do not flout their wisdom in other people's eyes, as though Sarasvatī was there, but concealing herself.

128. The wife of Śiva and daughter of the Himālaya mountains. She has two characters, one mild and the other fierce, and it is under the latter that she is especially worshipped. She has many forms. In her milder form she is Umā, 'light' and a type of beauty, Gaurī, 'the yellow or brilliant' and Pārvatī, 'the mountaineer'. In her terrible form she is Durgā 'the inaccessible', Kālī and Śyāmā 'the black', Caṇḍī and Caṇḍikā 'the fierce', and Bhairavī, 'the terrible'. As Durgā, she is a beautiful yellow woman riding on a tiger in a fierce and menacing attitude.

129. Wise men are charmed because of their devotion to the goddess Durgā, and the foolish ones because of fear of her.

130. Aditi literally means 'free, unbounded'. Infinity—'the visible infinite, visible by the naked eye; the endless expanse beyond the earth, beyond the cloud, beyond the sky.' (*Max Müller*). She is called the 'mother of the gods' and the 'mother of the world'.

Its loveliness
is as though Rati,[131]
taking a form,
had come to captivate
Kāma.

Adorned with all graces
and giving joy,
it is like Indrarānī[132]
whom learned men
praise.

48. Mūlan hī kī jahāṁ adhogati Keshav gāiye.
Hom hutāshan dhūm nagar ekai malināiye.
Durgati durgan hī ju kuṭil gati saritan hī meṁ.
Śrīphal ko abhilāsh pragaṭ kavi kul ke jī meṁ.

No one in Ajodhyā goes downward
except the roots of trees.
There's no pollution
save that caused by the smoke
of oblations.
No place is inaccessible
except fortresses
which foes can't reach.
No one moves crookedly
except rivers.
No one covets *śrīphal*[133]

131. Rati (see note 13).

132. Wife of Indra, and mother of Jayanta and Jayantī. She is also called Śacī and Aindrī, and is said to be the most fortunate of females, 'for her husband shall never die of old age'. Indra chose her for his wife from a number of competing goddesses because she surpassed them all in voluptuous attraction.

133. The word *śrīphala* is used in a double sense. It means either (i) wealth or (ii) the *bela* fruit—the Indian wood-apple. The wood-apple is a spinous tree with imparipinnate leaves, white flowers in loose racemes, with a fleshy fruit, having a hard, rough, woody rind. A transparent oily fluid exudes from the trunk of the tree when an incision is made into it, and is used by painters for mixing their colours. The tree also yields a

save the poets
for using it as a simile
for the breasts of women.

49. Ati chanchal jaṁh chaldalai, vidhavā banī na nāri.
Man moho rishirāj ko, adbhut nagar nihāri.

Only the *peepul* leaves[134]
are restless :
and there's no widow
save the forest,
because it is without
the *dhavā* tree.[135]

When Viśvāmitra saw
this wonderful city
his mind was charmed.

50. Nāgar nagar, apār, mahāmoh tam mitr se.
Tṛṣṇā latā kuṭhār, lobh samudra Agastya se.

Countless men live here,
who are as the sun
to dispel the darkness
of great ignorance :
or as an axe

clear white gum, and the wood is valuable for its durability, hardness, and whiteness. The fruit is eaten, and its soft core also used for preparing a sherbet which is said to have a cooling effect and to be beneficial to the stomach.

The poet says : 'No one in the city of Ajodhyā covets wealth (*śrīphala*), but the poets use it (*śrīphala* meaning the fruit) in their love-poetry to compare women's breasts to it.' Because of the hard kernel of the fruit and its roundness, Hindu poets sometimes liken women's breasts to it.

134. Pipal is the Indian ivy. It is a roadside tree with small verdant heart-shaped leaves giving good shade. The leaves are light and shake in the breeze, hence they are said to be restless.

135. A wild growing shrub. There is a pun here on the word *vidhavā* which means either (i) a widow or (ii) 'Deprived of the *dhavā* tree' (*vi*= 'without' or 'deprived of', and *dhavā*=the *dhavā* tree).

to cut the creeper
of desire :
or as the sage Agastya[136]
to soak
the ocean of greed.

51. Viśvāmitra pavitra muni, Keshav buddhi udār.
Dekhat shobhā nagar kī, gaye rājadurbār.

Says Keśavadāsa,
thus beholding
the splendour of the city,
the wise and virtuous sage,
Viśvāmitra,
proceeded to King Daśratha's
durbar.

The City of Mithilā (From Chapter 5)

Rāma and his brother Lakṣmaṇa, were taken by Viśvāmitra to kill the demons. They arrived in Mithilā, the capital of king Janaka's kingdom, after many adventures. The observations about the city which follow are made by the two brothers.

Lakṣmaṇa.

15. Chahuṁ bhāg bāg taṛāg.
Ab dekhie baṛ bhāg.
Phal phūl soṁ saṁyukt.
Ali yauṁ ramaiṁ janu mukta.

136. A *ṛṣi* who was born in a water-jar as a fish of great lustre, and at birth was less than a span in length. He acquired the name Pītābdhi or Samudra-culuka—'ocean-drinker', as he is believed to have drunk up the ocean because it offended him, and because he wished to help the gods in their wars with the Daityas when the latter had hidden themselves in the waters. He was afterwards made regent of the star Canopus, which bears his name.

What Lakṣmaṇa said

Brother Rāma, see,
tanks and groves abound
in Janaka's city.

The groves
are full of flowers and fruits
amid which the black bees
wandering,
are like saints going about
unrestrainedly.

Rāma

16. Ti na nagrī ti nā nāgarī, prati pad hansak hīn.
Jalaj hār shobhit na jahṁ, pragaṭ payodhar pīn.

What Rāma said

Janaka's kingdom
is replete with ponds full of water,
in which many swans live,
and clusters of lotuses
grow.

In his domain
all women wear toe-rings,[137]
and on their big breasts
pearl necklaces
dangle.

137. A toe-ring (*bichhia*) is a small silver ring worn on the toe or one of the fingers of the foot. Only married women wear toe-rings or any other ornaments. The implication is that there are no widows in Mithilā. The big breasts of the women denote that they are all healthy and cheerful.

The Hermitage of Bharadvāja (From Chapter 20)

After the long war with Rāvaṇa, the demon-king, was over, Rāma, accompanied by his brother and Sītā, departed for Ajodhyā. On the way they visited, amongst other things, the hermitage of sage Bharadvāja. In the verses which follow, Keśavadāsa describes the hermitage and the peace which reigns there.

34. Bhardvāj kī bāṭikā Rāma dekhī.
Mahādeva kī sī banī chitta lekhī.
Sabai vṛkṣa mandārahū te bhale haiṁ.
Chhahūṁ kāla ke phūl phūle phale haiṁ.

When Rāma saw
Bharadvāja's garden
he thought it to be Śiva's
because the trees in it
were more beautiful
than the *madār*.[138]

All the fruits and flowers
of the six seasons
were there.

35. Kahūṁ hansinī hansa syoṁ chitta choraiṁ.
Chunai os ke bunda kuktān bhoraiṁ.
Śukāli kahūṁ Śārikālī birājaiṁ.
Paṛhaiṁ Veda mantrāvalī bhed sājaiṁ.

Beautiful ganders and geese
move about
charmingly :
they peck at dew-drops
mistaking them for pearls[139]

138. The *madāra* or *mandāra* tree is the swallow wort plant having small round prickly fruit which are offered in worship to god Śiva. Hence the presence of these trees in Śiva's garden is what one would expect.

139. The *rājahaṁsa* is a kind of swan or goose with red legs and bill, sometimes compared to a flamingo. The geese living in the Mānasarovara lake and celestial places are believed to eat pearls and to have

Parrot and starlings
tunefully chant
the *Vedas*.[140]

36. Kahūṁ vṛkṣa mūlasthalī toya pīvaiṁ.
Mahāmatta mātang sīmā na chhīvaiṁ.
Kahūṁ vipra-pūjā kahūṁ deva-arcā.
Kahūṁ yoga-śikṣā kahūṁ Veda-carcā.

Intoxicated elephants
drink water from troughs
around trees,
but do not break
their branches.

All over the hermitage
priests are praying,
men are worshipping gods,
giving lessons in Yoga,[141]
and expounding
the *Vedas*.

37. Kahūṁ sādhu paurāṇakī gāth gāvaiṁ.
Kahūṁ yajña kī śubhra śālā banavaiṁ.
Kahūṁ homa-mantrādi ke dharma dhāraiṁ
Kahūṁ baiṭhi ke Brahmavidyā bicāraiṁ.

Sages recite Purāṇic verses[142]
and kindle the bright flames

the power of distinguishing between true and false ones. Here the geese in the sage's hermitage mistake the round dew-drops for pearls and so pick at them.

140. Celestial parrots and starlings are believed to have the gift of speaking like human beings, and so those in the sage's hermitage, being gifted with this power, recite the *Vedas* to perfection.

141. *Yoga* is from *yuj*='to join'. It is a school of Indian philosophy founded by Patañjali, and having eight steps for attainment, viz., self-control, religious duty, postures, control of breath, control of the senses, control of mind, meditation, and transcendental contemplation or ecstasy.

142. The Scriptures of the Hindus written in verse in the form of a dialogue. They are eighteen in number and deal with topics like the

of oblations:
men chant mantras,
and propound
the Vedānta.[143]

38. Suvā hī jahāṃ dekhiye vaktrarāgī.
Chalai pippalai tiksha budhyai sabhāgī.
Kampaiṁ śrīphalai-patra haiṁ yatra nīke.
Surāmānurāgī sabai Rāma hī ke.

The red juice of betel leaves
does not stain the lips
of dwellers in Bharadvāja's hermitage:
only the parrots there
are the red-mouthed ones:
the leaves of the *peepul* tree alone
are restless:
only the wisdom
of wise men
is sharp:
no one trembles (with fear)
save the plantain leaf:
and all men are filled
with Rāma's loves,
not that of a
woman.[144]

39. Jahāṁ vāridai vrinda bājāni sājaiṁ.
Mayūrai jahāṁ nityakārā birājaiṁ.

creation of the universe, its destruction and renovation, the genealogy of gods and patriarchs, the reigns of the Manus, and the history of the Solar and Lunar races of kings.

143. The third division of the *Vedas* attached to the *Brāhmaṇa* portion, and forming part of the *Śruti* or revealed word also known as the *Upaniṣads*. They are generally written in prose with verse in between, but some are wholly in verse. They discuss matters like the origin of the universe, the nature of the soul and the connection of mind and matter. They are therefore eminently philosophical in nature.

144. There is a pun here. *Rāmānurāgī* means (i) one who loves Rāma or (2) one who loves a woman (*rāmā*=woman, *anurāga*=love).

Bharadvāj baiṭhe tahāṁ vipra mohaiṁ.
Mano ek hī vaktra lokeśa sohaiṁ.

There's no music or dance
in this hermitage
except the rumbling of clouds
and the dancing of peacocks.

Bharadvāja,
Who sits here
charming the minds of Brahmins
by his readings from the scriptures,
seems like a one-mouthed
Brahmā.'[145]

Lakṣmaṇa

40. 'Keshodāsa' mrigaj-bachherū choshai bāghnīn,
Chāṭat surabhi bāghabālakbadan hai.
Singhan kī saṭā echaiṁ kalabh karani kari,
Singhan ko āsan gayanda ko radan hai.
Phaṇī ke phaṇan par, nāchat mudit mor,
Krodha na virodha jaham mad na madan hai.
Bānar phirat ḍore ḍore andha tāpasani.
Shiva ko samāj kaidhauṁ rishi ko sadan hai.

What Lakṣmaṇa said

How wonderful is this hermitage
where fawns drink the milk of tigresses,
cows lick the faces
of tiger cubs:
baby elephants
playfully pull the manes of lions
with their trunks,
lions sit fearlessly

145. Brahmā (see note 124), has four faces, hence known as *catur-mukha* (*catur*=four, *mukha*=face). Here the poet imagines that the sage Bharadvāja has the splendour of a Brahmā with only one face and the mouth.

on elephants' tusks:
and peacocks dance
on the hoods of serpents.

Here no one harbours
anger or opposition:
drunkenness and lust
are unknown.

Monkeys
hold ascetics by the hand
and guide them.
How astonishing!
Is this the abode
of Bharadvāja,
or of Śiva?

41. Jahūṁ komalai kalkalai vās sohaiṁ.
Jinhaiṁ alpadhi kalpaśākhī bimohaiṁ.
Dhare śṛṅkhalā dukkha dāhaiṁ durantai.
Manaum śambhujī sang līnheṁ Anantai.

There is no one delicate
in this hermitage
save the garments
made from the birch tree's bark
which ascetics wear.[146]
Even the Wishing Tree[147]
is envious of the hermits
clothed thus;
and is charmed by them.
They wear only loin-cloth and girdle,
but their strength is enough
to overcome
grievous sorrows.
They look like Śiva and Śeṣa
together.

146. Hermits, ascetics and sages living in the forests wore garments of the bark and leaves of the birch tree.

147. *Kalpaśākhī* or *kalpataru* or the Wishing Tree, is a mythological tree which is believed to grant all desires.

King Daśaratha's Elephants (From Chapter 1)

This interesting description occurs in the first chapter of the book, when sage Viśvāmitra is on a visit to Ajodhyā, along with his friends. Elephants were used in the armies of those days and so elephant stables were an essential section of the palace.

28. Jahṁ tahṁ lasat mahā madmatt.
Bar bāran bār na dal datt.
Ang ang charache ati candan.
Muṇḍan bhurke dekhiye bandan.

Intoxicated elephants
are chained in their stables,
looking magnificent.

They are so powerful
that they can trample even armies
in minutes.

There is sandal-wood paste[148]
on their limbs
and vermilion[149]
on their heads.

29. Dīh dīh diggajan ke Keshav manahuṁ kumār.
Dīnheṁ rājā Dashrath hiṁ digpālan upahār.

148. Sandal-wood, the scented wood of the sandal tree, is used in India primarily for religious purposes. When moistened with water and rubbed on a slab or disc of stone, it yields a thick paste with which Hindus anoint their foreheads, especially after a bath in a holy river. The paste, apart from sweetly scented, has a cooling effect. The limbs of elephants are smeared with this paste to beautify them as well as to keep them cool. Sandal-wood is also used in handicrafts and ornamental sticks. Cigarette boxes etc. are made of it.

149. Vermilion or mercuric sulphide power is a bright red pigment, which in the powdery state has a bright scarlet colour. It is used by Hindu married women for adornment, and is put in the line of parting of the hair, or as a round mark on the centre of the forehead. Mahouts also adorn the heads of their elephants with vermilion, which may seem rather strange, but then Hindi poets also compare the elegant gait of a woman with that of an elephant.

Says Keśavadāsa,
these elephants are so huge
that they seem to be the progeny
of the *diggajas*.[150]

Perhaps the guardian deities
of the eight points.[151]
have gifted them
to King Daśaratha.

The Ceremony of Palkāchār (From Chapter 6)

The ceremony of Palkāchār is prevalent in Bundelkhand, the area of Uttarpradesh which is towards Central India. The bridegroom, along with his friends, comes into the maṇḍap (a canopy raised for ceremonial purposes). There the bride and the bridegroom are made to sit on the same bed, and after they have done so, the friends and bosom-companions of the bride laugh and joke with them. The women of the city, too, find this a suitable occasion to see the bridegroom. In other states in India this ceremony is known as the Kumwar Kalevā.

Here the occasion is the wedding of Rāma, son of King Daśaratha of Ajodhyā, and Sītā, daughter of King Janaka of Mithilā. The princes, adorning themselves, and wearing fine clothes, have come into the maṇḍap, and have taken their places under the canopy according to their respective ranks and stations, and the Palkāchār ceremony begins.

38. Rāchī viranchi bās sī nithambarajikā bhalī.
Jahāṁ tahāṁ bichhāvane bāne ghane thalī thalī.
Vitān set syām pīt lāl nīl se raṁge.
Mano duhūṁ disān ke samān bimba se jage.

150. The eight mythical elephants, called *diggajas*, support the earth in the eight different directions. According to Hindu belief these elephants keep the earth intact. Their names are Airāvata, Puṇḍarīka, Vāmana, Kumuda, Añjana, Puṣpadanta, Sārvabhauma, and Supratīka.

151. The guardian deities of the eight points are the supporters of the regions. They support the eight points of the compass with the help of the *diggajas*, and are known as *Dikpālas*.

The pillars of the *maṇḍap*
are as magnificent
as those of Brahmalok.[152]

Under coloured tents—
white, black, yellow, red, and blue—
beddings of matching hues are spread;
so that it seems they are reflections
of the tents themselves.[153]

39. Gajmotin kī avalī apar.
Tahṁ kalasan par urmati suḍhār.
Subh pūrati rati janu ruchir dhār.
Jahṁ tahṁ Ākāśagaṅgā udār.

Garlands of elephant-pearls
dangle from pitchers[154]
placed in the *maṇḍap*;
which seems as though out of love
the heavenly Gaṅgā,
dividing itself into many streams,[155]
was flowing inside.

152. Hindus divide the universe into seven divisions (i) Bhūloka, the earth, (ii) Bhuvarloka, the space between the earth and the sun, the region of the *munis, siddhas* etc., (iii) Svarloka, the heaven of Indra between the sun and the polar star, (iv) Maharloka, the abode of Bhṛgu and the other saints, who are believed to be co-existent with Brahmā, (v) Janaloka, the abode of the sons of Brahmā, (vi) Tapoloka, where the *vairāgīs* (ascetics) reside, and (vii) Satyaloka or Brahmaloka, the abode of Brahmā, reaching which a being is absolved from further birth.

153. Meaning thereby that the beddings match with the colours of the tents. A yellow tent has yellow bedding in it, a red one a bedding of red colour, and so on.

154. Elephant gems or pearls are believed to be found in the heads of elephants. The illusion is purely figurative and fanciful because no such pearls have ever come out of elephant's heads. What is meant is that the garlands were made of very rare and costly pearls. Pitchers (earthen or of metal), are considered to be auspicious, and so placed inside the canopy. Sometimes women with earthen pitchers on their heads welcome a visitor on auspicious occasions.

155. The Ākāśagaṅgā is the celestial Gaṅgā or the Viyadgaṅgā which, according to the *Purāṇas*, flowed from the toe of Viṣṇu, and which was

40. Gajdantan kī avalī sudesh.
Tahṁ kusumrāj rājat subes.
Śubh nṛpkumārikā karat gān.
Janu devin ke puṣpak vimān.

From eaves[156]
all around the courtyard
beautiful flower garlands
dangle.

The balconies
on which princesses
sit and sing,
are like
flying chariots.[157]

41-42. It ut sobhit sundari ḍolāiṁ.
Arath anekani bolani bolaiṁ.
Sukh muke maṇḍal chittani mohaiṁ.
Manahu anek kalānidhi sohaiṁ.
Bhṛkuṭi bilās prakāshit dekhe.
Dhanush Manoj manomaye lekhe.
Charāchit hās chandrikani māno.
Sukh mukh bāsani bāsit jāno.

Lovely girls go about on the balconies,
laughing and jesting:
their charming faces
are like many moons,

brought down from heaven by the penances of sage Bhagīratha to purify the ashes of the sixty thousand sons of King Sagara, who had been burnt by the angry glance of Kapila.

The flashing pearl necklaces hanging from the pitchers are likened to the Ākāśagaṅgā—as though it had broken itself into so many streams and flowed inside the *maṇḍapa*.

156. *Gajadata* or *toṛā* is a piece of ornate woodwork shaped like a bird's beak, about two feet long, which is fixed projecting outside the wall of the house towards the roof to support the eaves. In a wedding, women sit on the eaves and sing, and watch the ceremonies going on below.

157. The gods and goddesses moved about in *vimānas* or flying chariots. The ancient counterpart of the aeroplane.

their eyebrows
like splendid bows
made from Kāma's mind,[158]
their laughter
vies with moonbeams, and
their mouth odour
is fragrant.

43. Amal kapolai ārasī, bāhui campakmār.
Avalokanai bilokiyo, mṛgmadamaya ghansār.

Their glistening cheeks
are as mirrors,
their arms
as garlands of *campā* flowers;[159]
the whites of their eyes
are as camphor, and
the pupils black
as musk.[160]

44. Gati ko bhāru mahāurai āṁgi ang ko bhāru.
Keshav nakh sikh shobhijai sobhāī singāru.

158. Kāma, or Kāmadeva, is the Hindu god of the love. He is the lord the heavenly nymphs (*apsarās*). He is armed with a bow and arrows. The bow is of sugar-cane, the bowstrings a line of bees, and each arrow is tipped with a distinct flower. He is usually represented as a handsome youth riding on a parrot and attended by nymphs, one of whom bears his banner displaying the Makara, or a fish on red ground. His wife is Rati, the goddess of desire, and a beautiful woman (see note 13). Kāma inspired the god Śiva with amorous thoughts of Pārvatī while he was engaged in austerities, and for this offence the angry god reduced him to ashes by opening his third eye. Śiva afterwards relented and allowed Kāma to be born again as Pradyumna, son of Kṛṣṇa and Rukmiṇī. He has a son named Aniruddha and a daughter, Tṛṣṇā.

159. *Campā* is the Spanish jasmine—a small flowery tree about ten feet high, with large smooth leaves. During the hot and rainy season it bears large corymbs of big white exquisitely fragrant flowers with the interior of their cups yellow.

160. The whites of the eyes are compared to camphor which is white in colour, and the black pupil to musk which is black. Eyes of Indian women have black pupils.

The girls are so delicate
that even the red dye[161] on their feet
seems to them a burden,
and so too their brassieres.

Says Keaśavadāsa, these girls
have no need to adorn their bodies,
for their loveliness itself
is adornment.

45. Baiṭhe jarāye jare pālikā par Rāma Siyā sab ko man mohaiṁ.
Jyoti samūh raho maṛhikai sur bhūli rahe bapuro nar ko haiṁ.
Keśav tīnahu lokan kī avaloki vṛthā upamā kavi ṭohaiṁ
Śobhan sūraj maṇḍal māṁjh mano Kamalā Kamalāpati sohaiṁ.

Sitting on the ornamental bed,
Rāma and Sītā captivate
the hearts of everyone:
they are surrounded by
lovely girls.

Even gods are perplexed
when they see their splendour,
how much more
poor men.

161. The red dye made from lac is used by married Hindu women for colouring the hands and feet. A bride's feet are invariably dyed with it, and it is used on all auspicious occasions and on festivals and ceremonies. Chauras, a writer of the first century, speaks of 'women's reddened feet on which anklets jingle'. Describing the hurried exit of ladies from their lovers' arms, the Sanskrit dramatist Murāri says: 'Footprints on pavements of moonstone, marked with the love that dyes deep the feet, wet with drops that have the radiance of rising cream, made with anxiety at each step as the *cakora* fly up disturbed, mark the departure of ladies who violate decorum'. In *Gīta Govinda*, Kṛṣṇa colours Rādhā's dainty feet with lac, and in *Kādambarī* the dyed feet of a Caṇḍāla woman are described thus : 'The rich lac on her lotus feet was like Durgā's feet crimsoned by the blood of Asura Mahiṣa she had just trampled on'.

Mother and Son (Indian Sculpture)

[to face p. 147

Says Keśavadāsa, poets may search
vainly for a comparison
in all the three worlds:
but to me it seems they are
as though Lakṣmī and Nārāyaṇa[162] seated
on the splendid orb
of the sun.

The Sorrows of Childhood, Youth and Age (From Chapter 24)

Rāma came back to Ajodhyā after having rescued Sītā and destroyed the army of demons. His years of banishment were over and he began to rule as king and to enjoy the pleasures of the palace. Here in the twenty-fourth chapter of Rāmacandrikā Keśavadāsa relates the sorrows af childhood, youth and age, from an interesting angle.

(*A*) *The Sorrows of Childhood*

3. Poch bhalī na kachhū jānai.
Lai sab bastun ānan ānai.
Śaiśav te kachhu hot baṛe ī
Khelat haiṁ te āyān chaṛhe ī.

Children do not distinguish
between things good and bad
but put them all in their mouths,
and when they are older
they unwisely spend
all their time
playing.

162. Nārāyaṇa is another name for Viṣṇu, the second god of the Hindu triad--the Preserver. In the *Mahābhārata* and the *Purāṇas*, Viṣṇu is called Nārāyaṇa, 'moving in the waters', and is represented pictorially in human form slumbering on the serpent Śeṣa, and floating on the waters. His consort is Lakṣmī, goddess of fortune. Sometimes he is represented seated on a lotus with Lakṣmī beside him, or reclining on a leaf of that plant. Lakṣmī is said to have four arms, but is generally shown as having only two, and holding a lotus in one hand. She is famed for her grace and beauty.

4. Haiṁ pitu mātan teṁ dukh bhāre.
Śrīguru te ati hot dukhāre.
Bhūkh na pyās na nīṁd na jovaiṁ.
Khelan ko bahu bhāṁtin rovaiṁ.

They are vexed
when their parents
burden them with work,
or when their teachers
teach them.

They forget
hunger, thirst, and sleep,
and care only for
play.

(*B*) *The Sorrows of Youth*

5. Jārati chitta citā duchitāī
Dīha tvachā ahi kop chabāī.
Kāmasamudra jhakorani jhulyo.
Yauvan chor mahāmad bhulyo.

Misgivings
perplex the young man,
anger
confounds his mind.

He tosses restlessly
on passion's sea,
and is intoxicated
by the power of his
youth.

6. Dhūp se nīl nicholani sohai.
Jāye chhuī na vilokat mohai.
Pāvak pāpśikhā baṛ vārī.
Jārati hai nar ko parnārī.

The youth burns
with adulterous desire

Anxious for the Beloved
(From an old painting by Molaram)

[to face p. 148

for another woman.[163]
His temptress, Lust,
is like a girl
wearing a smoke-blue
dress.

He cannot fulfil his craving
due to fear
of social opprobrium,
and keeps yearning
from afar.

(C) *The Sorrows of Old Age*

11. Kaṁpai ur bāni ḍagai bar ḍīṭhi tvachā 'tikuchai sukuchai mati belī.
Navai navgrīva thakai gati Keshav bālak te saṁgahī saṁg khelī.
Liye sab ādhin byādhin sang jarā jab āvai jvarā kī sahelī.
Bhagai sab deh dashā, jiya sāth rahai duridauri durāśā akelī.

His voice trembles,
his sight
is unsteady,
wrinkles appear on his skin,
and his wisdom
has declined.

He walks now
with bowed neck,
and tires
soon.

163. *Paranāri* can mean either (i) another man's wife whom the youth wishes to enjoy, or (ii) a *Parakīyā* i.e. a married woman who is in love with another person. In that case the youth would have the love and assent of the woman which would make enjoyment of her easier.

When Old Age,
Death's companion,
comes to dwell
in the old man's body
along with all bodily and mental ills,
his limbs lose their strength:
only vain hope
remains.

12. Viloki śiroruh set samet tanoruh kobid yoṁ guṇa gāyo.
Uṭhe kidhauṁ āyu kī audhi ke ankur śūl ki śuṣk samūl nasāyo.
Jaraiṁ kidhauṁ Keshav vyādhin kī kidhauṁ ādhi ke ākhar ant na pāyo.
Jarā sar pañjar jīva jaryo ki jarā jarkambar soṁ pahirāyo.

Seeing the gray hair
on his head,
and all over his body,
learned men say:

'Are these sprouts
of approaching Death?
or has the inert Soul
been pricked all over
with dry thorns?

'Perhaps these are
the roots of some disease,
or countless letters
of mental anguish
inscribed
on his forehead.

'Or has Old Age
imprisoned the Soul
in a cage of arrows?
or covered him
with a shawl
embroidered with silvery threads?'

Age and Youth (By Abanindranath Tagore)

[to face p. 150

The Game of Polo (From Chapter 29)

It is doubtful if polo was played in the time of Rāma, but it certainly was in Keśava's time. It seems the players rode on elephants as well as on horses while playing it, for in the second verse of this chapter (not translated) the poet says: 'Whomever Rāma orders, rides the horse or the elephant pointed out by him'. Thus, taking time off from his kingly duties, Rāma, his brother Bharata, and other princes, are pleasurably engrossed in this popular game.

5. Ek kod Raghunāth udār.
Bharat dūsrī kod vichāra.
Sohat hāthe līnheṁ chharī.
Kārī pīrī rātī harī.

On one side there's the munificent Rāma,
on the other Bharat, his brother:
they carry sticks
of different colours to play with;
black, yellow, red, and green.

6. Dekhan lago sabai jagjāl.
Ḍāri dayo bhuv golā hāl.
Golā jāi jahāṁ Jahṁ jabai.
Hot tahīṁ titahī tit sabai.

The people of the city
are watching the game.
The ball has been placed
upon the ground,
and wherever it goes
all the players follow
in a moment.

7. Mano rasik locan ruci race
Rūpa sang bahu nācāni nace.
Loka lāj chhāṛe aṁg-aṁg.
Ḍolat jan manu jāyā sang.

The players
run with the ball,
as eyes of amorists
turning instantly
towards
beautiful girls:
or as a man
going with his wife[164]
not caring at all
for what people may say.

8. Golā jāke āge jāye
Soī tāhi chalai apanāye.
Jaise tiyagaṇa ko pati rayo.
Jehi pāyo tāhī ko bhayo.

Whoever gets the ball
carries it towards the goal
as an adulterous husband
delays not to take a girl
who falls for him.

9. Utate it itāte ut hoi.
Nekau ḍhīl na pāvai soi.
Kāma krodha mad maṛho apār.
Jaise jīva bhramai saṁsāra.

Continually moving to and fro,
the ball is never still:
'tis as the wandering
of the raging and lustful soul
in the world
of existence.

10. Jahāṁ tahāṁ māre sab koya.
Jyoṁ nar panch-birodhī hoya.

164. In Indian society of Keśava's time it was not considered proper for a man to go publicly with his wife. Women were confined to the inner apartments.

Gharī-gharī prati ṭhākur sabai.
Badalat bāsan bāhan tabai.

Wherever it goes
the ball is hit by the players;
as the opponent of the *panch*[165]
is disgraced
everywhere.

The princes who are playing,
frequently change their garments,
and the horses or elephants
they ride upon.

11. Jab-jab jītaim hāl Hari, tab-tab bajat nishān.
Haya gaya bhūṣaṇa bhūri paṭ, dījat logani dān.

Whenever Rāma wins the goal
musical instruments are played,
and horses, elephants,
ornaments, and clothes,
given in charity.

Rāma's Bedchamber (From Chapter 29)

After King Rāma had sat late through the night in his council his intimate friend Shuk, came and requested him to end his durbar and rest in the palace. Poet Keśavadāsa tells us how Shuk persuades Rāma to retire for the night, and goes on to describe the bedchamber.

165. The Pañcas are the elected members of the village council whose function is to settle small disputes in the village and manage its property to the best advantage. The head of the council is called a *sarpañca* or village headman. Since the *pañcas* are respectable men of the village anyone who opposes them will be bound to be met with censure and disapproval.

Shuk

20. Pauṛhiye kripānidhān, devadeva Rāmacandra,
Candrikā samet candra, raina citta mohai.
Manahu suman-sumati sangu, ruche ruchir, sukrit rang,
Ānaṁdmaya ang-ang, sakal sukhan sohai.
Lalit latan ke bilās, bhramarvṛnda 'havi udās,
Amal kamal-kosha āspās bās kīnheṁ.
Taji-taji māyā durant, bhakta rāvare ananta
Tava pada kar nain, bain mānahu man dīnheṁ.

What Shuk said

The night has far gone
O god Rāma,
end your durbar now
and sleep.

The moon shines tonight
as the pure, buoyant, and blissful mind
of a wise man
who has done noble deeds.

The swarms of black bees
abandoning beautiful creepers,
and hovering around lotus clusters,
are like your countless devotees
forsaking the inscrutable *māyā* [166]
and meditating
on your feet, hands, eyes, and face.

21. Ghar-ghar sangīt gīt, bājat bājaiṁ ajīt,
Kāma bhūp āgam janu, hot haiṁ badhāye.

166. *Māyā* 'illusion', is the unreal appearance of nature, the phenomenal cloak or covering of the Absolute, which is not real but exists in appearance only. When this cloak is removed, realization is obtained. But the task is difficult, and here the poet imagines that the devotees, having given up this difficult quest, now turn their minds towards Rāma, and this turning round is like the abandonment by black bees of the creepers and their swarming around the lotus buds.

Rājbhaun āspās, dīpavṛkṣa ke vilās,
Jagat jyoti yauvan janu jyotivant āye.
Motinmaye bhīti naī candra candrikāni maī,
Pank-ank ankit bhava bhūri bhed vārī.
Manahuṁ śaśi paṇḍit kari, jānha jyoti maṇḍit śrī
Khaṇḍ shail kī akhaṇḍ shubra darīsārī.

The strains of music
coming from every house
are as songs
to greet the god of love.

The glimmering tree-shaped lamp stands[167]
are as bodies of young girls
glowing
with the onset of youth.

The new walls
inlaid with pearls
bear designs in sandal-wood paste
of all things in the world:

The moonlight shines on them;
craftily entering
the rooms of the palace,
which are grand as the Malaya hills,[168]
to serve King Rāma.

22. Ek dīp duti vibhāti, dīpati maṇi dīp pāṁti,
Mānahu bhuvabhūp tej mantrin maya rājai.
Āre maṇikhacit khare, bāsan bahu bās bhare,
Rākhit grah-grah anek manahu main sājai.

167. A huge stand of wood or metal, shaped like a tree, having small niches for lighting oil-lamps. On such a stand hundreds and thousands of oil-lamps could be lit. In those days such tree-shaped lampstands were kept in big mansions and palaces.

168. The Malabar Hills, the south part of the Western Ghats. Ordinarily the moon's light does not penetrate inside caves of mountains, but here because of the desire to serve Rāma the Moon has by her cleverness managed to send her rays even inside the big halls of the palace which are lofty as the Malaya mountains.

Amal, sumil, jalanidhān, motin ke śubh vitān,
    Tāmahṁ palikā jarāya, jaṛit jīva harshai.
Komal tāpai rasāl, tansukh kī sej lāl,
    Manahuṁ soma sūraj pe, sudhāvindu varṣai.

The gems set in the walls,
scintillating
in the light of the single lamp
seem as ministers
glorying
in the king's splendour.

The lovely gem-studded jars
filled with perfumed things,
kept in niches
in every room,
are as articles
for Kāmadeva's use.

Under a canopy
of white, glimmering, and even, pearls,
there's a bedstead
laid with precious stones,
which looks most pleasing
with a lovely mattress
of red satin.

The pearls
which fringe the awning
over the bed,
are like drops of nectar
dripping
from the moon to the sun.

23. Phūlan ke vividh hār, ghorilan ormat udār,
    Bich-bich maṇishyām hār, upamā Shuk bhāshī.
Jītyo sab jagat jāni, tumasoṁ hiya hār māni
    Manahu Madan nij dhanu teṁ, gun utāri rākhī,

Jal thal phal phūl bhūri, ambar paṭbās dhūri,
Svachha yakṣakardam hiya, devan abhilāeṣ.
Kumkum medojabādi, mṛgamad kapūr ādi,
Bīrā banitan banāya bhājan bhari rākhe.

Flower garlands of many kinds
and sapphire necklaces
hang from pegs
in the bedroom:

as though, Shuk says,
having conqured the entire world,
but admitting defeat from Rāma,
Kāmadeva had taken off
the string from his bow
and hung it.

All kinds of flowers and fruits
of land and sea are there;
perfumed powders
to put on clothes,
yakṣakardam,[169]
the cosmetic
for which even gods
crave,
and perfumed
saffron pastes.

Women have filled
betel-boxes
with betels
scented with camphor
and musk.

169. A kind of cosmetic paste made by grinding together camphor, aloe wood, musk, and a kind of gourd.

The Bedstead (From Chapter 30)

Having described the bedroom in which Rāma is going to sleep, Keśavadāsa goes on to describe the bedstead in the room.

12. Phūlan ke suvitān tanyo var.
Kanchan ko palikā yak tā tar.
Joti jarāye jā'yo ati śobhanu
Sūrajmaṇḍal teṁ niksyo janu.

The bedstead of gold,
studded with gems,
glimmers
under a canopy of flowers,
as if it had just emerged
from the sun.

13. Darsat hī nainan ruchi banai.
Basan bichhaye sab sukh sanai.
Ati suchi sohaiṁ kabahuṁ na sunyo.
Janu tanu lai kai sasi kar chunyo.

The bed's bright splendour
can only be seen;
it is indescribable.

The pleasing bedcover
is of such dazzling whiteness,
that it seems
the moon had been flayed
and its skin
spread.

14. Champakdal duti ke geṁḍue.
Manahu rūpa ke rūpak uye.
Kusum gulāban kī galsuī.
Baraṇi na jāyaṁ na nainan chhuī.

The pillows
have the hue of *campā* flowers[170]
the small, soft, rosy, cushions
for resting the cheeks,
cannot be described,
for the very contact of sight
would soil them.

The Science of Government (From Chapter 17)

Rāma's army crossed the sea and entered Laṅkā (Ceylon) to wage war against Rāvaṇa. The battle raged fiercely. Rāvaṇa sent his son, Indrajit, when he found that Aṅgada, a warrior on Rāma's side, was playing havoc with his forces. Indrajit spread a dark screen around Rāma and Lakṣmaṇa so that they were cut off from the main army, and then sent the Snake Noose Dart after them. The snakes lashed themselves round the two brothers. While they were in this predicament, the vulture-god Garuḍa, came and released them. Thereafter many warriors on Rāvaṇa's side were slain. Seeing this Rāvaṇa called his advisor, Mahodar, and asked him for his counsel. The advice given by Mahodar is contained in the lines which follow. Since Keśavadāsa was intimately connected with the Orchhā durbar, and through it with the Mughal Court, his views on statecraft are of particular significance. First he enumerates the various kinds of kings, and then the different types of ministers and advisors.

20. Kahyo Śukrācārya su hauṁ kahauṁ jū.
Sadā tumhāre hit sangrahauṁ jū.
Nṛpāl bhū meṁ vidhi chāri jānauṁ.
Suno mahārāj sabai bakhānauṁ.

170. Spanish jasmine (See note 159). The comparison is particularly apt because Rāma and Sītā are known as 'lotus-shaped', and when they sleep on cushions of the colour of *campā* flowers, black bees, which are normally attracted to lotuses, will not attack their faces for they never swarm round *campā* flowers.

What Mahodar said to Rāvaṇa

I'll recount to you
what Śukrācārya told me,
for I ever desire
your well-being.

Listen,
there are four kinds
of kings
on this earth.

21. Yahai lok ekai sadā sādhi jānai.
Balī benu jyoṁ āpu hī Īśa mānaiṁ.
Karai sādhanā ek parlok hī ko.
Hariścandra jaise gaye dai mahī ko.

Some kings
concentrate their efforts
on this world,
thinking it to be the only one:
as Bali[172]
who thought himself to be God.

171. Śukra or Śukrācārya (the planet Venus) was son of Bhṛgu and priest of Bali and the Daityas. His wife was Suṣumā. He performed a penance by imbibing the smoke of chaff with his head downwards for a hundred years. His mother was killed by Viṣṇu whom Śukra cursed 'to be born seven times in the world of men. Śukra restored his mother to life, and the gods being alarmed lest his penance should be accomplished, sent Jayantī, Indra's daughter to lure him, but he completed his penance and married her. He is also known as Bhārgava, Bhṛgu, and Kavi or Kāvya 'the poet'.

172. Bali was a good and virtuous *daitya* king. His grandson was Prahlāda, a devotee of God and a virtuous man. Through his devotion and penance he defeated Indra, humbled the gods, and extended his authority over the three worlds. The gods appealed to Viṣṇu for protection who came to Bali as a dwarf and craved from him the boon of three steps of ground. Having obtained the boon he stepped over heaven and earth in two strides, but out of respect for Bali's kindness and because of Prahlāda's virtues, stopped short, and left to him Pātāla, the infernal regions.

Others
recognize only the other world,
as Hariścandra[173]
who gave away the earth
in charity.

22. Duhūṁ lok ko ek sādhaiṁ sayāne.
Videhīn jyoṁ bed bānī bakhāne.
Naṭhaiṁ lok doū haṭhī ek aise.
Trishankai haṁsai jyoṁ bhaleū anaiṁse.

Some are so shrewd
that they subdue
the two worlds:
as the Videha kings[174]
mentioned in the *Vedas.*

Some are so headstrong
that they annihilate
both worlds:

173. The story of Hariścandra is mentioned in the *Aitareya Brāhmaṇa*, *Mahābhārata* and the *Mārkaṇḍeya Purāṇa*. One day while he was hunting he heard female lamentations which came from the Sciences who were being mastered by sage Viśvāmitra. Being a defender of the distressed, he went to their rescue, but Viśvāmitra was so provoked by his interference that the Sciences immediately perished and Hariścandra, on the sage's asking, promised to give him everything he asked. Viśvāmitra stripped him of all his wealth and kingdom. His wife and child were sold and he was reduced to a state of abject poverty. Dharma came in the guise of a Caṇḍāla and employed him to steal shrouds from a cemetery. There he met his wife who had gone to cremate her son. After many hardships the gods interceded on his behalf and he ascended to heaven leaving his son to govern the kingdom. From there he was expelled, because induced by the sage Nārada, he boasted of his merits, but as he was falling he was forgiven, and his downward course arrested. He and his followers dwell in an aerial city, which, according to popular belief, is still visible occasionally in mid-air.

174. Videha was an ancient country, of which the capital was Mithilā, corresponding to modern Tirhut or North Bihar. The *Vedas* mention it. King Janaka of Videha was one of the greatest of kings. His adviser was the sage Yājñavalkya. He asserted his right of performing sacrifices without the intervention of priests, in which he succeeded because he became a Brahmin through his pure and righteous life.

as Triśaṅku,[175]
whom all men,
good and evil,
deride.

23. Chahūṁ rāj ko maiṁ kahyau, tumso rāj caritra.
Ruchai su kījai citta meṁ, chintahu mitra amitra.

I have thus narrated
the attributes
of kings of all the four kinds:
now whether you take me to be
your friend or foe,
consider well
and do as it pleases you.

The Kinds of Ministers (From Chapter 17)

24. Chāri bhāṁti mantrī kahe, chāri bhāṁti ke mantra.
Mohi sunāyo Śukra jū, sodhi, sādhi sab tantra.

What Mahodar said to Rāvaṇa

After consulting all the books of wisdom
Śukra has told me
that there are four kinds of ministers
and their counsels too
are of four kinds.

175. A king of the Solar race, descended from Ikṣvāku, father of Hariścandra. He was a pious king, and was desirous of performing a sacrifice in order to ascend bodily to heaven. With great difficulty he persuaded Viśvāmitra to perform the sacrifice, and Triśaṅku (also called Satyavrata) ascended to heaven. But the gods resisted this, and as a compromise it was agreed that he should be an immortal and hang with his head downwards and shine among some new stars. This is the account given in the *Rāmāyaṇa*. The *Viṣṇu Purāṇa* and *Harivaṁśa* give slightly different versions.

25. Ek rāj ke kāj hataiṁ nij kāraj kāje
Jaise Surath nikāri sabai mantrī sukh sāje.
Ek rāj ke kāj āpane kāj bigārat.
Jaise locan hāni sahī kavi balihiṁ nivārat.
Ik prabhu samet apno bhalo, karat dāsrathi dūt jyoṁ.
Ik apno aru prabhu ko burā, karat rāvaro pūt jyoṁ.

What Mahodar said

Some ministers sacrifice
the good of the realm
for their own gain,
as those who banished
King Surath.[176]

Some bear hardships
for their king,
as Śukrācārya
lost an eye
to deter Bali.[177]

176. The story of Rājā Suratha is mentioned in the *Mārkaṇḍeya Purāṇa*. It is related that the king gave all the affairs of state to his ministers, and would himself always be engaged in hunting. The ministers, considering him to be ignorant, removed him from the kingdom.

177. (See note 172). The reference is to an incident mentioned in the *Purāṇas*. Śukrācārya was the preceptor of Bali, the *daitya* king. When Bali defeated Indra, the king of the gods, the gods appealed to Viṣṇu for protection. Viṣṇu came to Bali in the form of a dwarf and craved from him the boon of three steps of ground. Śukrācārya cautioned Bali that it was Viṣṇu in the form of a dwarf and asked him not to grant him the boon as the god wanted to take away his kingdom by deceit. But Bali said that if the dwarf was Viṣṇu it was his good fortune to be blessed by his sight. So he gave him the boon. The dwarf, Vāmana, who had come to outwit Bali, stepped over heaven and earth in two strides, but out of consideration left Bali the Pātāla region. Bali brought a spouted jug filled with water for Vāmana to offer as oblation. Seeing that his disciple's kingdom would be lost Śukrācārya compressed himself into the spout of the jug. Vāmana guessed that he was there, and asked Bali to clean the spout with a twig. When Bali did so the twig pierced Śukrācārya's eye and he lost it.

Some,
like Hanumān, [178]
bring good
to their rulers
and to themselves:
others,
like your own son, Meghnād,[179]
bring evil.

26. Mantra ju cāri prakār ke, mantrin ke je pramān.
Vish se dāṛim bīj se, guṛ se nīṁb samān.

What Mahodar said

Know for certain
that the counsels given by ministers
too,
are of four kinds—
like
poison,
pomegranate seed,
jaggery, and
neem.[180]

178. Hanumān proved very helpful to Rāma in tracing out and recovering Sītā. Also thereby he won eternal glory and immortality for himself.

179. The reference is to the incident in which Hanumān, the monkey god, and warrior of Rāma's army, was sent to Laṅkā to get news of Sīta. He despoiled the demon king Rāvaṇa's groves and arbours, and so Meghanāda, Rāvaṇa's son, was sent to deal with him. Meghanāda bound Hanumān, and when he was taken before the demon king, he got his tail set fire to. This enabled Hanumān, to burn the city of Laṅkā, which, as a result, was razed to the ground. Therefore by his action of binding Hanumān, Meghanāda did great harm both to himself and his king, Rāvaṇa.

180. The four kinds of counsels are compared here to these things for the following reasons : poison is disagreeable in eating and destroys life, therefore counsel of this sort is disagreeable and noxious: pomegranate seeds are sweet in taste and nourishing, hence counsel of this kind is sweet and strengthening: jaggery is sweet but causes loose stools, hence counsel of this sort is sweet of nature but causing trouble: last of all *neem* is bitter but removes disease, so counsel of this kind is bitter but happy in the result.

27. Rājnīti mat tatva samujhiye.
 Desh-kāl guni yuddha arujhiye.
 Mantri mitra ari ko guṇa gahiye.
 Lok lok aplok na bahiye.

What Mahodar said to Rāvaṇa

Consider, my lord,
good government to be the consensus
of public opinion:
 then pondering well
 whether the time is favourable,
 and the people;
 begin this battle (against Rāma).

One should accept
good counsel,
whether it is from a minister or friend,
or from a foe;
 to avoid disrepute
 in this world
 and in the next.

Precepts For Kings (From Chapter 39)

The thirty-ninth chapter of Rāmacandrikā contains Rāma's advice regarding politics and his tips about good government. After having distributed his kingdom between his nephews, sons, and grandsons, prior to retiring from kingship, Rāma goes on to give all of them advice about how they should conduct themselves, so that they can govern their kingdoms well. This chapter shows Keśavadāsa's intimate knowledge of statecraft, which he had acquired by being close to the Orchhā rulers, and through them to the Mughal Court. After having taught them the art of good government, Rāma narrates how a ruler should protect his kingdom.

29. Boliye na jhūṭh īṭhi-mūṛh pai na kījie.
Dījiye ju vastu hāth bhūli hū na lījie.
Nehu toriye na dehu dukka mantri mitra ko.
Yatra tatra jāhu pai patyahu jaiṁ amitra ko.

What Rāma said

Don't speak lies,
and do not befriend
a fool.

Do not even by oversight
take back what you have given
to another.

Do not withdraw affection
after having once bestowed it.
Do not aggrieve
a minister or friend.

Go to foreign lands,
but do not trust
a foe.

30. Juvā na kheliye kahuṁ jubān Veda rakṣiye.
Amitra bhūmi māhiṁ jaiṁ abhaksha bhaksha bhakshiye.
Karau na mantrh mūṛh soṁ na gūṛh mantra kholiye.
Suputra hohu jaiṁ haṭhī maṭhīn soṁ na boliye.

What Rāma said

Do not ever gamble.
Preserve the *Vedas*.
Be cautious about what you eat
in an enemy country.
Do not accept the counsel
of an ignorant man.
Do not disclose
your secret designs
to anyone.

Sons,
abandon stubbornness;
and do nothing to provoke
the abbots
of monasteries.

31. Vrāthā na pīṛiye prajāhi putra mān pāriye.
Asādhu sādhu būjhikhai yathāparādh māriye.
Kudeva deva nāri ko na bāl vitta lījiye.
Virodh vipra vansha soṁ su svapnahū na kījiye.

Do not harass your subjects
needlessly,
treat them like your sons:
discriminate
between the innocent and the guilty
when giving punishment.
Do not appropriate the wealth
of a priest, a god,
a woman or a minor:
and do not ever oppose
Brahmins.

32. Par dravya ko to viṣ prāya lekho.
Paristrīn ko jyɔṁ guru istrīn dekho.
Tajau kāma krodhau mahāmoh lobhau.
Tajau garva ko sarvadā chitta chhobhau.

Treat as poison
another's wealth.
Look on another man's wife
as you would on your mother.
Abandon
vanity, lust, greed, delusion
anger, and agitation.

33. Yashai saṅgrahau nigrahau yuddha yodhā.
Karau sādhu saṁsarga jo buddhi bodhā.
Hitū hoya so deijo dharma śikṣā.
Adharmīnko dehijaiṁvāk bhikshā.

Amass renown.
Subjugate enemies.
Keep the company of wise sages.
Consider religious teaching beneficial,
and do not converse with
unrighteous men.

34. Kritaghnī kubādī paristrī bihārī.
Karau vipra lobhī na dharmādhikarī.
Sadā dravya sankalpa ko rakṣi lījai.
Dvijātin ko āpu hī dān dījai.

Do not appoint officers
who are ungrateful, blashphemous,
adulterous, or greedy,
for dispensing
charity.

Distribute
money set aside for Brahmins
with your own hands,
prudently.[181]

181. The reference is to an account of a king of the name of Satyaketu who was a very powerful and munificent ruler. He appointed a Brahmin for distributing money and wealth as charity. This Brahmin would appropriate the greater part for himself and give only a nominal sum to those to whom the charity had to be distributed. Once it so happened that king Satyaketu went along with his army to wage war in a foreign country, where he was killed. The messenger of Yama, the god of Death, took him and presented him before the god who asked him whether he would first suffer the consequences of the sins he had committed on the earth, or get the rewards of his good deeds. The king was wonder-struck to hear this and said, 'I don't remember having committed any sins'. Yama then told him about the Brahmin he had employed, and of how he misappropriated the greater part of the sum which he was given to distribute as charity, and spent it for his own pleasures in giving it to prostitutes and women of ill-fame. Thus the virtuous king had to suffer the consequences of his carelessness in entrusting the work of charity to the wicked Brahmin. Rāma therefore, exhorts his sons and nephews to keep this work in their own hands.

Methods to Protect the Kingdom (From Chapter 39)

35. Terah maṇḍal maṇḍit bhūtal bhūpati jo kram hī kram sādhai.
Kaisahu tākahṁ śatrun mitra su Keśavadāsa udās na bādhai.
Śatru samīp, pare tehi mitra, su tāsu pare juṃ udās kai jovai.
Vigraha, sandhini, dānanisindhulauṁ lai chahuṁorani to sukha sovai.

What Rāma said to His Sons and Nephews

No enemy, ally, or neutral power,
can harm a king
who has arranged well
thirteen kingdoms,[182]
including his own.

He should wage war
with the kingdoms next to his,
maintain peace
with those lying further,
and exchange gifts
with those on the outmost limit.

The king who organises
his kingdom with others
thus,
right till Sindh,[183]
sleeps contentedly.

182. The thirteen kingdoms are, one which is the king's own, and on all the sides, east, west, south, and north, three each; making thirteen in all. By keeping enmity with the adjoining kingdoms the people in the king's domain are always alert—hence this policy is beneficial.

183. The province of Sindh towards the north-west of India, which is now in Pakistan.

36. Rājshrī bash kaisahūṁ, hohu na ur avadāt.
Jaise taise āpubash tākahṁ kījai tāt.

What Rāma said

Above all
O magnanimous sons and nephews,
do not be blinded by kingly power:
achieve glory
by restraint.

BIBLIOGRAPHY

English

1. FARQUHAR, J., *Outline of the Religious Literature of India* London, 1920.
2. MACNICOL, Nichol, *Indian Theism*, London, 1915.
3. DUTT, M. N., (Tr.), *The Rāmāyaṇa*, Calcutta 1892-94.
4. DUTT, R., *The Rāmāyaṇa*, London, 1926.
5. GRIFFITH, R. T. H., (Tr.), *Vālmīki Rāmāyaṇa*, 5 vols., London, 1870-74.
6. SEN, M. L. (Tr.), *The Rāmāyaṇa*, 3 vols., Calcutta, 1929.
7. ṢHASTRI, H. P., *The Rāmāyaṇa of Vālmīki*, London, 1950.
8. RAYCHAUDHRI, H., *Materials for the Study of the Early History of the Vaishnava Sect*, Calcutta, 1936.
9. BHANDARKAR, D. R., *Some Aspects of Ancient Indian Culture*, Madras, 1940.
10. DURANT, W., *The Story of Civilization*, New York, 1935.
11. MORGAN, K.W., (Ed.), *The Religion of the Hindus*, New York, 1953.
12. WINTERNITZ, M., *A History of Indian Literature*, 2 vols., Calcutta, 1963.
13. GRIERSON, G. A., *Linguistic Survey of India*, 11 vols., Calcutta, 1906.
14. ALTEKAR, A. S., *Sources of Hindu Dharma*, Sholapur, 1953.
15. BARNETT, L. D., *Hindu Gods and Heroes*, London, 1922.
16. SIVANANDA, Swami, *Hindu Gods and Goddesses*,1956.
17. CHAKRABERTY, D., *Cultural History of the Hindus*, Calcutta.
18. DOWSON, J., *Classical Dictionary of Hindu Mythology and Religion*, Routledge, London, 1961.
19. MALINOWSKI, B., *Myth in Primitive Psychology*, London, 1936.
20. PILLAI, G. K., *Hindu Gods and Hidden Mysteries*, Allahabad, 1958.
21. WALKER, Benjamin, *Hindu World*, 2 vols., Allen and Unwin, London, 1968.

Hindi

22. GUPTA, D. S., *Keśava Kāvya Manovaigyānika Vivecana*, Regal, Delhi, 1968.
23. PRASAD, J., *Keśavadāsa*, Vinod Pustak Mandir, Agra, 1966.
24. VARMA, K. C., *Ācārya Kavi Keśavadāsa*, Sahitya Prakashan, Delhi, 1957.
25. SHARMA, K. C. *Keśavadāsa Jīvanīkalā*, Bharatiya Sahitya Mandir, Delhi, 1961.
26. SHUKLA, K. S. *Keśav kī Kāvya-kalā*, Pustak Sadan, Varanasi, S. 2014.
27. BHATNAGAR, R. R., *Keśavadāsa ek Adhyayan*, Kitab Mahal Allahabad, 1947.
28. CHAUHAN, R. G. S., *Keśava Aur Rāmacandrikā Punarmūlyāṅkana*, Vinod, Agra, 1967.
29. SHARMA, S. S., *Ācārya Keśavadāsa*, Hindi Sansar, Delhi, n.d.
30. SINGH, Vijaipal, *Keśava Aur Unakā Sāhitya*, Rajpal, Delhi, 1961.
31. SINGH, Vijaipal, *Keśavadāsa*, Radhakrishna Publication, Delhi, 1970.
32. SINGH, Vijaipal, *Keśava Sudhā*, Rajpal, Delhi. 1969.
33. AYYAR, Vishvanath, *Keśavadāsa*, Lok Bharti, Allahabad, 1967.
34. PRASAD, J. K., *Keśavadāsa*, Vinod, Agra, 1966.

INDEX

ERRATA

Page	*For*	*Read*
77	lightening	lightning
103-117 in the Heading	Rāmā's Maid-servants	Sītā's Maid-servants